CW00407672

A MILLENNIAL MOMENT

Bikram Vohra joined *The Illustrated Weekly* in 1969 after graduating from Loyola College, Chennai, and went on to become Resident Editor of *Sunday Standard* and *Indian Express*, Mirzapur, Ahmedabad, at the age of twenty-seven. His schooling years, he describes to his kids as having been exemplary, though the truth is a bit different. He was first published at the age of seventeen, and his first regular column appeared when he was twenty-two. He anchored a TV show in India for fourteen years and was much in demand as an emcee and motivational speaker. After running *Navhind Times* in Goa, he came to the Gulf in 1984 to relaunch *Gulf News*, as its managing editor. He has had four tenures at *Khaleej Times* as editor, editor of *City Times* and as consultant. He has also helped in setting up *Gulf Today*, worked with *Times of Oman*, served as editor of *Bahrain Tribune* and a consultant with *Arab News*. His column in these papers was called 'Between the Lines' and had a passionate following. He is also a recognized aviation writer and ran the *Middle East Aviation Journal* for ten years, as well as the afternoon paper *Emirates Evening Post*. He also worked in the media section of the United Nations. His first love in writing is to make for happy laughter, the sound of which he sees as the saving grace of humanity.

He currently has a column of that genre in *Times of India*. He has written six books and an anthology of his funny haha funny peculiar columns was published in 2019 (*Between the Lines*, Xponent Media).

He has had over 22,000 articles published in over fifty newspapers worldwide and has covered wars, climbed mountains and been part of air accident investigations.

An avid squash player, he once stole a point from world champion Jahangir Khan and took a lap of honour. He lives in Dubai with his family in situ—one wife, two daughters, two sons-in-law, four grandchildren, Daisy the spaniel, Toby the tortoise, an army of stray cats and a partridge in a pear tree.

A MILLENNIAL MOMENT

A Mandir in the Middle East Transforming History and Hearts

Bikram Vohra

PENGUIN
ENTERPRISE

An imprint of Penguin Random House

PENGUIN ENTERPRISE

Penguin Enterprise is an imprint of the Penguin Random House group of companies whose addresses can be found at global.penguinrandomhouse.com

Published by Penguin Random House India Pvt. Ltd
4th Floor, Capital Tower 1, MG Road,
Gurugram 122 002, Haryana, India

First published in Penguin Enterprise by Penguin Random House India 2024
Published in Penguin Enterprise by Penguin Random House India 2024

Copyright © Swaminarayan Aksharpith 2024

All rights reserved

10 9 8 7 6 5 4 3

The views and opinions expressed in this book are the author's own and the facts are as reported by him which have been verified to the extent possible, and the publishers are not in any way liable for the same.

ISBN 9780143467366

Typeset in Adobe Caslon Pro
Printed at Thomson Press India Ltd, New Delhi

This book is sold subject to the condition that it shall not, by way of trade or otherwise, be lent, resold, hired out, or otherwise circulated without the publisher's prior consent in any form of binding or cover other than that in which it is published and without a similar condition including this condition being imposed on the subsequent purchaser.

www.penguin.co.in

*'Some moments freeze in time
and some moments freeze time;
they are singular moments that bring
minds, hearts, and humankind together;
they are "Millennial Moments" that
redefine history and celebrate the
harmony of humanity.'*

Swami Brahmaviharidas

Contents

विदेश मंत्री
भारत

Foreword

The establishment of the BAPS Hindu Mandir in Abu Dhabi has a significance far beyond the immediate event. It is a statement of centuries of cultural, social and economic contacts between Bharat and the Gulf. It is equally an expression of the understanding and empathy that has underpinned the relationship between our peoples. Most of all, it is a message for the future about how the wisdom and vision of leaders can help realise the goal of Vasudhaiva Kutumbakam, the world as one family.

In 1997, His Holiness Pramukh Swami Maharaj prophesied that a Mandir of historic significance would arise in the region. The realization of this dream began in 2015 when Prime Minister Narendra Modi met with UAE President HH Sheikh Mohammed bin Zayed al Nahyan. From their understanding, a project took shape that has now reached its culmination. And that endeavour embodies the UAE President's conviction that 'we are all brothers', as it does the Prime Minister's belief in one earth, one family, one future. At a time when the world is beset by conflict, uncertainty and parochialism, the Mandir has emerged as a clarion call for peace, humanity and international understanding.

The construction of the Mandir has been the labour of love for countless saints, volunteers and workers. They have been motivated by the spirituality of His Holiness Mahant Swami Maharaj. The BAPS

172, South Block, New Delhi-110011 Tel : 91-11-23011127, 23011165 E-mail : diream@mea.gov.in

Sanstha in UAE under the guidance of Swami Brahmaviharidas put its heart and soul in this endeavour, not pausing even during the challenging times of the Covid pandemic. Today, we see the cumulative results of the devotion and commitment of so many to this noble enterprise.

Such a momentous happening deserves to be recorded and retold, especially for the generations to come. I am therefore very pleased that Bikram Vohra has undertaken that responsibility through the publication 'A Millennial Moment'. I commend his efforts to share various aspects of the making of this BAPS Hindu Mandir with the world. I join many others who see in its inauguration the fulfilment of a personal commitment.

S. Jaishankar

(Dr. S. Jaishankar)

172, South Block, New Delhi-110011 Tel : 91-11-23011127, 23011165 Fax : 91-11-23011463
E-mail : diream@mea.gov.in

Preface

When I was fourteen, I sulked for three continuous days in an effort to emotionally blackmail my father into buying me a long-playing record of *Summer Holiday*, a series of pop songs sung by Cliff Richards. It was for ₹33, and that was a lot of money then. The year was 1963. When I finally got it, I felt peculiarly vindicated. Like I deserved it. By much the same persuasion, a few months later, the film *The Great Escape* starring Steve McQueen hit the movie screens. In those days, there was no telephonic reservation possible so having thrown a tantrum, I forced my father to drive through torrential monsoon rain to the theatre, some 15 kilometres away, and then drive all the way back at night through even more drumming sheets of water. These two acts of teenage self-indulgence clearly had a significant impact on me and nearly sixty years later, are still startlingly vivid. In many ways, they formatted my value system as I looked back at these events some years later, mortified by this brattish behaviour.

As a distillation of the adult guilt over my two indiscretions and a pubescent failure to acknowledge the life of extreme privilege I was leading, I gradually lost interest in expensive things. It wasn't a sackcloth and ashes thing, not by a long shot. I still love caviar, 80-inch TV screens, hardcover books, high-end colognes and creature comforts. Conversely, I have no interest in expensive cars, designer clothes or branded shoes. Paying exorbitant prices for a meal in a restaurant leaves me in gloom for days. I would love to travel at the front of the plane, but I cannot afford it. Food plays a nominal role in my day. If it is there, I will eat it. The bric-a-brac in our home are not collector's items, nor are the paintings on our walls worth a princely ransom. I would be happy with a cheap knockoff of a mobile phone, but I adore my Kindle.

This mindset has the hallmark of confusion stamped on it. There is a dichotomy here, as if I was picking and choosing my preferences and was more hypocritical than ascetic. I could be accused of this pretence since life has never been bad. On the contrary, I do believe someone up there likes me and yanks me back from the brink when things look bleak. Perhaps because it has happened so often, I have never planned for the future—no nest egg, no cushion, nothing to break the potential fall. Been saved but never saved.

I also like to be kind. In an obvious, upfront way. It gives me great pleasure to help people even though I know I am being conned. The 'You're a better man than I am, Gunga Din' is a valid syndrome. My spurts of generosity are not selfless; they pander to my ego, and I enjoy the homage of the grateful. Yet, I will walk a mile for the underdog. Go figure! The weaker, the poorer, the needier, the further I will walk. If that is the sort of humility that conceals a great vanity, so be it.

Pampered by the fates and having dodged bullets right through my career, now in my mid-seventies, I discover there are people who get off the gravy train, who leave behind pelf and power, career and comfort to walk a path so lofty and often lonely. Most of us are denied that unique capability.

I never got off the nine-to-five treadmill. I fought it like I fought dogma and mediocrity all my life but stayed on them. If there is a regret I have, it is that the fifty-one years of newspapering in twelve different companies were all short-circuited by unpleasant intent and broken promises and the refusal to bend a principle—those awful restraints that emanate from your own value system. I have never been given a farewell speech, a cake at a farewell or a memento to mark my tenure.

That is not regret; it is humour, that wonderful saviour of the human race often given such little importance . . . the right to happy laughter.

Humour is my cheerful bow and arrow; when I saw it flourishing in such abundance in my first meetings with the *swamis* of Bochasanwasi Akshar Purushottam Swaminarayan Sanstha (BAPS) Swaminarayan persuasion, it left me perplexed. Who were these people in saffron robes who laughed and were not sepulchral and ponderous? They spoke in British and American accents and joked, and there was very little of that heavy, intimidating spiritual browbeating that one associates with religion. That guilt-trip orchestrated to subdue, not energize.

Just an insight into the minds of these swamis and their global personae; a wide range of careerists who have been Managing Directors (MDs) and Chief Executive Officers (CEOs) and leaders of commerce and business and finance, professors, corporate honchos, students, men of art and science who shut shop and said, 'Here we are, ready to serve, task us.'

I was initially chary. As I got to know them better and read up on the history, what hit me hard, besides the humour and genial cordiality, was the fact that they had all got off the gravy train and walked into a celibate life sans all possessions and even blood relationships. They had all dumped their careers, cast away money and position and were incredibly happy to serve their God and his devotees.

What really struck me forcefully was the dedication of the volunteers. They get no reward in fiscal terms, and yet, they come in their thousands to render service not for a couple of hours, but for years. They give their time, spend their own money and are there to be reckoned with.

My halfway-house approach to material things pales in comparison. This is the real McCoy, and it requires great commitment and belief. It was here, while spending time at the centenary celebrations of Pramukh Swami Maharaj of Bochasanwasi Akshar Purushottam Swaminarayan Sanstha (BAPS) in Ahmedabad in January 2023, that I was intrigued enough to want to write this book from a non-religious angle without beating any deliberately favourable drums.

So, unsure of the terrain I was entering, I spoke to a very special friend who has also been one of my closest allies. A devout and more religious person than Ashok Puri is difficult to find. In the days of old, when we were all tiptoeing nervously into underplayed *kirtans* and muting the volume, he was holding *bhajan* sessions with much aplomb and no apology. Even today, he has a *mandir* at home, one in his office and definitely a third in his heart. Blessed with a voice that is captivating, his largesse is incomparable. A man who runs schools for the underprivileged seemed like the right sort of person to obtain an opinion from.

'Ashok,' I said, 'what do you think, should I give it a shot?'

He didn't take long to answer. 'Do it,' he said, 'you have been given a sign, don't ignore it.'

Let this book be seen and read in the same vein of happy humour and good feeling that the *sanstha* so passionately promotes. A revelation of a faith whose sinews are forged in crucibles of high thought and a search for that elusive divine truth.

Several people helped me in this year of writing, paramount among them Swami Brahmaviharidas who helped me in this saga by giving me time, but with the proviso that this was *my* book and not something commissioned by BAPS. 'Tell your story, relate your experience with complete independence,' he said. 'If we commission it, then it becomes a PR exercise, for which I could have hired anyone from among a thousand choices. No, you do it your way.'

That was both a blessing and a heavyweight of responsibility. In many ways, he had imposed the sanstha's value system on me—be totally honest and transparent, say it as you see it, warts and all.

For sheer eloquence bathed in good sense, Swami Brahmaviharidas is a veritable titan. They don't make many of them.

I fell back for encouragement and more knowledge on Swami Aksharatitdas, a man who gave up a fast-track career and became a sadhu and is an incandescent influence on those who can grab his attention. I have always enjoyed his company and conversation, and it is these two swamis who bookended me into continuing whenever I faltered or lost my way.

In the middle of the exercise, I was introduced to a high-profile educationist from the UK, who had elected to take a sabbatical. Umesh Raja does not set himself to music but back in Britain's schooling system, a whole orchestra could play hosannas for him. He became my sounding board, willingly or unwillingly, I am not so sure, but I stole his time shamelessly day and night, intruding upon his privacy often thoughtlessly. For that indiscretion, I hope I am forgiven. I see him as a friend, and I can only hope it is reciprocated.

Later in the process, one man who had an impact on this work was a successful travel expert from the UK. Nitin Palan fetched up one day a bundle of frenzied energy and began pushing buttons. For him, time was of the essence and sitting around waiting was not an option. I have to say he did galvanize any tardiness in the schedule with his 'move it, what are we waiting for?' approach to things.

From day one, I had an understudy. This young man, a student from the USA, has been of such enormous help and support, and has shown so much patience with my inconsistencies and moods, that I do owe him a lot. Thanks for being there, Harikrishna Patel, right through the effort. You da man.

I must thank two ladies who set me straight on the role of women in the Swaminarayan context and removed some, till then, very concrete concerns. Thank you, Sonali and Chanda, for the clarity you provided when I brought up the prickly-pear notion of the position of women in BAPS. Your honesty and depth of thought were enlightening and endorsed the fact that as much as 60 per cent of volunteers and devotees of Bhagwan Swaminarayan are women, and they are energized, inspired and visibly proud of this religious allegiance. They understand the willpower and sacrifice it takes to become a sadhu and exercise restraint; one that demands walking the straight and narrow path to God without distraction.

These two ladies compelled me to wander further into this subject and reopen a chapter in the book. I do not dwell on it too much largely because the more one explains the more defensive one sounds, and the position of eminence and respect women hold in BAPS is reflected naturally across its activities, thereby making a lengthy discourse unnecessary, even impolite.

Another person who, without really realizing it, gave gentle nudges couched in pranks has been the ever-smiling Yogi Bhatt. He always made me feel like he was rooting for me. In the future, I hope he will take my calls.

And then there is Ashok Kotecha, without whose guidance, support and unflinching surrender to my impositions, my association with BAPS would not have been possible. You talk good people, you talk Ashok. He has been rock solid, and his courtesies are imprinted in my mind. His counsel has been priceless.

Many of those who gave their time and contributed tangibly are mentioned in the narrative. Their cooperation and acceptance of my interpretation of their words and ideas is humbling.

In the beginning, my family were faintly amused at my affection for a religious entity. They were more attuned to the husband and father writing about aviation and the armed forces, politics and the human condition, not the holy and the spiritual. But gradually, they took to the rhythm of the writing.

Finally, one odd event. I had been given some books on Bhagwan Swaminarayan and Pramukh Swami and three of these moved most mysteriously to the door of the little mandir in our home. No one took responsibility for the act, especially since the books were in different places.

When I mentioned this to Swami Brahmaviharidas, he just smiled. Enigmatic.

And if you can smile like so by the time you come to the end of this book, it will all have been worth the effort of writing it.

PART ONE

WHO ARE THEY?

1

These Extraordinary People

'In the joy of others, lies our own.'
—*His Holiness Pramukh Swami Maharaj*

This is an incredible story. It is a story about constructing a major Hindu temple complex in an Islamic nation and how it all happened. It is about extraordinary people setting a new standard in inclusivity, as seen through the eyes of an ordinary person.

I am that ordinary person. Untutored but sincere, a typical Indian with reasonable privilege who goes through life paying honest lip service to faith and hoping God will understand there just wasn't time enough to chant, pray and meditate.

How does one set about writing a book on a subject about which one knows very little? Much like no one has more right to become a saint than the sinner, perhaps no one has more right than the novice to take a plunge into the unknown and see things from a completely different perspective.

And so I thought, let's start at the very beginning—that is certainly a good place to start. As you walk with me through these words, you might find the same comfort and solace, even a beam of fresh awareness, that came to me from engaging in this exercise.

It is 3 April 1781—Chaitra *sud* 9, Samvat 1837, as per the Hindu calendar. Bhagwan Swaminarayan is born in Chhapaiya, a village near Ayodhya, in the present-day Indian state of Uttar Pradesh. 1781 is the year Uranus, the seventh planet, was discovered. It would become known as the Great Awakener. The Sun and Mercury are in conjunction that day, promising great ideas. The Moon and Neptune are in consonance, indicating grand spirituality. Pluto promises a high level of empathy. The stellar constellation signals the birth of a person with great integrity and honesty, backed by divine will.

It will all come true. So very true as Bhagwan Swaminarayan (1781–1830), also known as Sahajanand Swami, is believed by followers to be a manifestation of Purushottam, the Supreme Divinity, around whom the Swaminarayan Sampradaya developed. Today, he is worshipped by millions around the world, and millions live according to his teachings.

To dare to write a knowledgeable narrative on the persona that is Bhagwan Swaminarayan, or to even attempt to encapsulate the genius and incandescent impact of Pramukh Swami Maharaj, his fifth spiritual successor, would be a conceit. Much has been written by scholars and swamis, and much more will be written.

But for the many hundreds of thousands of us who are curious, more than just interested—even drawn to the movement of the Bochasanwasi Shri Akshar Purushottam Swaminarayan Sanstha (BAPS)—the need to understand what makes them tick is paramount. I ask myself, who are these people, where do they come from, where do they belong and what do they do? More importantly, where are they going? The Swaminarayan Sampradaya has been flourishing for almost 250 years, with BAPS emerging in 1907, and ever since, the organization has carved a remarkable path. Dedication, unwavering faith and tireless spiritual and social efforts have propelled BAPS to grow into a vibrant global movement, enriching the lives of countless individuals from diverse backgrounds, across generations. Yet, as I embark on this exploration, I find myself feeling my way in relative darkness, so I may be forgiven the indiscretion.

Hinduism is a vibrant tapestry of countless different traditions with a vast variety of beliefs and practices. The purpose of life for Hindus is to achieve four aims, called *purusharthas*. These are *dharma*, *artha*, *kama* and *moksha*. They provide Hindus with opportunities to act morally and ethically and lead a good life. These values are strongly reflected in the philosophy and ethos of the Swaminarayan religion, which says: 'The basic concepts of service, tolerance, faith, love for God and his ideal devotee Aksharbrahma, ever-presence of God, supremacy of God, form the core of Swaminarayan philosophy and practice.'* All very good reasons for BAPS, one of the leading Hindu traditions to be chosen for creating history in the Middle East by being given the opportunity to construct a majestic mandir here. So, what is that special texture in its fabric that distinguished BAPS to lead this landmark project in inclusivity, tolerance and forward-thinking governance?

---

* Sadhu Vivekjivandas and Sadhu Amrutvijaydas, *Basic Concepts of Swaminarayan Satsang* (Swaminarayan Aksharpith: Ahmedabad, 2007).

Based on the Vedic principles revealed by Bhagwan Swaminarayan, BAPS was formalized by Shastriji Maharaj (1865–1951), his third spiritual successor, and inspired by Pramukh Swami Maharaj (1921–2016). It is currently led by Mahant Swami Maharaj. This is how it introduces itself. Founded on the pillars of practical spirituality, it reaches out far and wide to address the spiritual, moral and social challenges we face in our world. With 1,600 temples around the world and over 5,000 active centres, BAPS has a few million devotees, 100,000 volunteers and 1,000 ordained swamis engaged in cultural, spiritual, educational, environmental, medical, social and other causes.

This book explores the human stories of the people behind this pathbreaking project and is also a record of the milestones that were crossed after permission was sought and granted for construction in Abu Dhabi, the capital of the UAE. Its construction will be a miracle and must be seen globally as a coming together of two nations and two major religions in peace, harmony and the promise of prosperity of the body and the soul.

As a person who has run newspapers in this region for the past thirty-seven years and seen how the rules of engagement in media have changed, the news that a massive Hindu edifice would rise in the confines of the capital was first met with genial disbelief. Naysayers for years had said, it would not be possible, that it was a bridge too far even for a progressive government such as the UAE.

Devotees recall that in 1997, Pramukh Swami spontaneously envisioned and prayed for a temple in Abu Dhabi while sitting on a sand dune in Sharjah. Later, his followers told him it was in the realm of a pipe dream and far away from reality.

Yet, despite the deep doubt, the miracle occurred, and on 14 February 2024, the magnificent mandir, set on 27 acres of land graciously gifted by the royal family, was inaugurated and opened to the public.

How it happened and things fell into place suggests a divine intervention in bringing together those whose generosity of spirit superseded all else.

I decided then that this saga deserved to be written; for posterity to know that in the twenty-first century, people of good faith existed and lived in the United Arab Emirates and India. That the world, despite the turmoil, did become a better place through this temple and the extraordinary people who made it happen: His Holiness Pramukh Swami Maharaj and his divine prayer, His Highness Sheikh Mohammed bin Zayed Al Nahyan and his generosity, Honourable Prime Minister Narendra Modi and his integrity, His Holiness Mahant Swami Maharaj and his spiritual purity and the thousands of volunteers, workers and well-wishers who made the impossible, possible.

2

The First Glimmers of Understanding

'When you want something, all the universe conspires in helping you to achieve it.'
—*Paulo Coelho*, The Alchemist

Before I could describe the incredible efforts that were made to make this dream a reality, it was necessary for me to attempt an understanding of the psyche of the BAPS and its philosophy. This was really a start from a point of rampant ignorance. I saw this absence of knowledge as a clean slate, with no preconceived notions and no pressure from any association or involvement of any individual. To me at this time, BAPS was just a label without any significance.

Drenched in blissful ignorance, but still a professional journalist, I packed curiosity and cynicism in equal measure and, thus went armed into battle. It so happened that the one-month-long centenary celebrations of Pramukh Swami Maharaj (referred to as PSM100), the fifth of six gurus in Bhagwan

Swaminarayan's spiritual succession, were being held at a specially designed location—a thirty-minute drive away from Gandhinagar, the state capital of Gujarat—from 15 December 2022 to 15 January 2023. In order, the other gurus in the lineage of Bhagwan Swaminarayan have been Gunatitanand Swami (1784–1867), Bhagatji Maharaj (1829–97), Shastriji Maharaj (1865–1951), Yogiji Maharaj (1892–1971), Pramukh Swami Maharaj (1921–2016) and Mahant Swami Maharaj—the current head of the organization. This was the ideal occasion to see for myself what BAPS was all about and why it had won the day against what many of us believed were great, even impossible, odds.

It is no surprise then that I willingly, even eagerly, accepted that invitation to the Nagar, the 600-acre mini-township in Ahmedabad created to mark and celebrate this incredible Swami's birth centenary. Farmers willingly loaned their land for a period of two years to create this complex without asking for anything in return. Over 80,000 volunteers made this township and played host to over 12 million visitors over thirty days. Just the children's pavilion displaying young talent attracted 4 million kids, and for the uninitiated like myself, that joyous, free-spirited, chilled-out atmosphere was quite contrary to my expectations. I have always felt that practitioners of religion are a little dark, a trifle humourless; more solemn and forbidding. This is so untrue where these swamis and their volunteers are concerned.

I am casually guarded. To be brutally honest, like most of us, I have a pleasant, loping but not very deep relationship with God and the rituals of worship. I am god-fearing, perform the occasional incantation, remain solemn and sober on my infrequent visits to a house of worship and can sit and be courteous and well-mannered at a prayer meet, while my thoughts tend to stray to other places. I mean no disrespect, quite the contrary, but I do not know the difference between prayer and *mantra*. I can mumble *shlokas* and say 'Om Namah Shivaya' with fervour, vigorously shout 'Jai Mata Ji' on the road to Vaishno Devi and recite the Gayatri mantra 108 times on my parents' death anniversary and feel comforted. Translating its intrinsic meaning would be a difficult exercise and one I tackled only recently, as I took the initial baby steps as a guest into the hallways of spirituality with the BAPS exercise. Just recently, I sang 'Raghupati Raghav Raja Ram' tunelessly but with gusto, and I felt good.

In aviation, it is called the angle of attack (AOA), the attitude of the aircraft when it takes off or approaches the runway. My AOA in placing one word after another is entirely different from those saintly scholars who have written deeply researched tomes on Bhagwan Swaminarayan or spent years walking behind Pramukh Swami, bearing witness to his immense largesse and sensitivity to the 'plights of the common man'. That phrase so often condescending in its tonal value, for once suits my AOA. Venturing into this strange yet fascinating, aspirational but intimidating world of total and unquestioning surrender to what the believers see as a calling and a valid way of life, I am a common man, a very common man. Trying, as I have said, in my own way, to capture the essence of extraordinary people from the eyes of an ordinary man—one whose priorities are far too brittle to find solace in such total immersion in faith.

I find confidence in the advice of Swami Brahmaviharidas, the 'go-to' sant for the Abu Dhabi temple and a towering personality in himself. He is warm, disarming, eloquent and has a tangible presence. One can feel that quiet strength, that sense of assurance that very few people have and can carry so lightly and effortlessly. 'You write it your way,' he says gently. 'Say what you feel, share that honesty with your reader; that is what will make this book special.'

It is a benediction in many ways, but it also intensifies the sense of responsibility. Whenever I have been in his presence, enjoying his erudition and his wit, I come away better for it.

3

Getting off the Treadmill

'Why were so many people committed to Pramukh Swami?
Because he was so committed to them.'

—*Swami Brahmaviharidas*

What makes these young people with advanced education, admission to Ivy League universities, top-of-the-pile jobs and plentiful material wealth, just stop riding along the career path? They dismount from that bicycle and walk away from it all without looking back. Now, a group of them stands in the North Indian winter dusk with this journalist, exulting over the fact that their saffron-coloured cotton throwover cape and the dhoti wears out faster on the elbow and the seat of the lower garment. To extend the life of their clothes, they were able to rejoin the better pieces and create a fresh attire. Their joy in this discovery is almost childlike and its rendition by four swamis touches my heart and I ask again, 'Who are you that saving a piece of cotton cloth is a source of such tangible satisfaction?'

Many of them—not just a few of the 1,100 swamis in the BAPS ranks—could have been the big pieces of cheese in the rat race, seen by their peers as symbols of success in the arts and sciences, in business and the corporate sector, in education, as bankers and technical titans; they cheerfully let that rope go.

Huge sacrifices, indeed. Each of the swamis I spoke to frown that word away. It is no sacrifice, it is a benediction, an opportunity to serve God on earth and keep the soul pure and unsullied by worldly rust.

So I ask myself, who is the quintessential symbol of BAPS? Is it a young man who will not identify himself because to do so is to seek publicity that detracts from his commitment? During the preparations for PSM100, with the temperature crossing 40°C, his role is to clean out the human waste from the bathrooms daily. With no golf carts at his disposal, he covers the 600-acre campus on foot to clean all of the bathrooms. At this stage, they do not yet have any drainage systems in place, so he would drain the waste holes manually. His father had passed away a few years ago, and his elder brother is working in Canada. It is just him and his mother, yet nothing could stop him from giving back to his guru, His Holiness Pramukh Swami Maharaj, who has given him everything. It is not even penance; it is pure love. He wants to serve. No one is forcing him.

Perhaps this symbol is young Dhruv, a guide from Uttar Pradesh at the Swaminarayan Akshardham temple in New Delhi, who escorts guests and has all the facts on his fingertips. Twice, I try to give him a tip and twice, he refuses. The third time, it is just him and I, so I pull out a ₹500 note, tell him to take it; no one is here, watching. He smiles wryly and says, 'You don't really understand, do you? I do this out of love for

Pramukh Swami. By taking money, the service would be ruined, I will not touch any sum.'

My designated driver during the PSM100 event, Mr Pande, had taken leave from his job to be a volunteer at the Nagar without even thinking of compensation. I ask him how he is going to manage the month with no income. He says, 'What greater honour than serving Pramukh Swami Maharaj; this is a blessing, we are all the richer for it.' He smiles and pats me on the shoulder and says, 'Money is not everything; the peace of mind we get from being volunteers is priceless.' He is not alone—there are 79,999 others doing exactly what he is doing by making themselves available. They are manning the roads, guiding traffic, driving golf carts, cooking 240,000 wholesome meals a day, assisting the visitors and creating a supply chain that is seamless and would make an army in action proud.

We all know that it is customary when you are being driven that you let your inhibitions slack a little and get chatty. So, I ask Mr Pande how his wife feels about being excluded from the volunteering since women are not allowed.

He says this is untrue and sets about setting me straight. 'It is not that women are disallowed,' he explains, 'but women do not come in the close proximity of the swamis, who have taken a vow of celibacy. That does not stop them from being devotees or taking active part in the arrangements. Would it surprise you to know that 60 per cent of the volunteers here are women and probably more than that percentage comprise the crowds coming in every day, because they look up to and venerate Pramukh Swami? If women felt rejected, they would not come in such great numbers.'

The point is well taken. It was in my mind, and I would have brought it up with the swamis anyway, but Mr Pande put things into perspective. I might bring it up again because there are still some people who feel there is a gender bias within the sanstha, and all the explaining in the world cannot overcome that. But I feel satisfied.

I don't know where the art piece finally ended up, but at the Nagar, a huge world record-holding portrait of Pramukh Swami was created by 150 women devotees from the UK using bubble wrap injected with different pastel colours, with not one bubble bursting. For that month it was one of the most popular exhibits attracting an average of 400,000 visitors every day.

Right through my stay, I recognize a highly developed sense of organization within the volunteers. Their logistics and admin are excellent, and it is a system that the private and public sector could emulate to their great advantage.

Conversely, I see the Nagar on the day after the event has come to closure. There are withdrawal symptoms in those dismantling, though even that is done with a certain courtesy and affection. Thousands of men, women and children have worked over a year, totally absorbed by this celebration, and suddenly, it is over, and they are visibly at a loss.

Later, I sit for over an hour with Avi, born and brought up in the US, aged twenty-one, with the world at his feet. He is two days away from leaving for the rigorous training of seven years to become a swami, and he is excited and exuberant. I say, 'Shouldn't you be out there on campus having fun, going to parties, living it up?' He shrugs and says, 'Been there, done that; all I got was a sense of wastefulness, an emptiness that now must be fulfilled by a commitment to my new life, a life of duty and service following the words of my God, Bhagwan Swaminarayan.'

'But you are giving up everything.'

'That is what you think. I am giving up nothing, instead I am getting so much, I am humbled.'

I, too, am humbled. And still not fully able to grasp the power and the glory of what these people do and what motivates them.

A group of young men joins us. They are on their way back to the USA on a flight the next day. They are all volunteers who had flown in to spend their winter break volunteering at the Nagar and are thoroughly enjoying themselves. Not for them the Caribbean or Florida or a flight across the pond to London. They are intrinsically no different from hundreds of other undergrads as they jape and joke and kid around with each other, except when they go back stateside to New Jersey, they will continue to serve by becoming builders. The Swaminarayan Akshardham in Robbinsville, New Jersey, the second-largest Hindu temple in the world. While the facilities are open for Sunday assemblies and festivities, the traditional temple itself is not completed. These young volunteers are taking part in its completion, stone by stone, piece by piece, even though they have no prior knowledge or experience of construction. Again, giving a whole new meaning to the phrase 'labour of love'. Their depth of engagement was seen in the way they attended the evening *arti* in the smaller temple. It was a natural flow of spiritual energy.

Since January 2022, young women over the age of eighteen have been volunteering for the temple construction in Robbinsville and engaging in bending rebars (reinforcement bars) on special machines. Their team consists of forty women. It is tough, demanding work. I talk to Krishna Patel, and she says it requires five people to curve the rod to a 45° angle, needing extreme physical pressure. On a site that is 180 acres in size, there are over 350 women volunteers who work on various aspects of the project. Women who are students, professionals and mothers, have taken time out of their lives for three months, six months, one year—some even opting to stay until completion.

When any of the volunteers at the New Jersey Akshardham tell you they have helped build the mandir, they mean it in the most literal sense. Everything from cutting and levelling concrete to placing the 10-tonne stones onto the mandir. Not one of them had even 1 per cent prior experience in this field, but through their devotion to their guru and God, they have achieved the impossible. This is the magic of Robbinsville Akshardham; it brings together people to do the impossible, to give back to society and to create an everlasting landmark of their faith. Empowered by their guru for their guru.

That evening, I am with a group of young swamis. They explain to me that they wear similar slippers which often get mixed up. So now they tattoo their initials onto the base to ensure they have taken the right pair. Several dozen times a day, they go through this ritual of removing footwear because shoes are not permitted inside the temple anywhere and can only be worn on the paths outside. It is the little things that produce joy and satisfaction. You don't have to buy a house to feel accomplished, not when your initials on the front of your slippers suffice to give you that mental boost.

They also greet each other by bowing down and touching feet. This is not just reserved for those elder than them, but even the youngsters do it to each other. In the beginning, a stranger to it all is bemused, but then it is explained that respect needs to be mutual and so the courtesy has a universal application, and age is not a bar.

'It is also good exercise,' says a swami with a wink.

There is a trait I notice occurring more frequently. There is a good deal of kidding around and laughter everywhere—humour has a role to play here.

'Got to exercise,' says another. 'Putting on weight not good.'

In the temple, after the evening arti, they prostrate full-length on the floor, which is not easy, especially for the elderly, but they all do it a minimum of five times a day.

You find that all the swamis are endearing, with their patience, their politeness and their readiness to listen to not just you but to anyone who approaches them.

Take the three directors of the Abu Dhabi project. Madhusudhan Patel, Sagoon Patel and Ullas Shukla. Their involvement is surreal. As is the toil of Sanjay Parikh, one of the senior architects of the temple. Sagoon is seventy-five years old and has two extremely successful sons. He had retired and was starting to cultivate his herb garden in London, when the joy of retirement was eclipsed by a greater calling. Fate decreed that he must pick up the baton in adverse circumstances. He received a call that Jasbir Singh, the project's previous director, had passed away, and his expertise in building mandirs was needed. That was exactly a year ago. Sagoon could not refuse the dictate and instantly came onboard. Madhusudhan was in America, running a motel development business, when he got a call. He did not question it and just dropped everything to come to Abu Dhabi. Ullas, who was a senior vice president at Reliance with at least five years left to keep earning good money, came of his own accord. He was driven by the belief that he had to give something back to society. He dropped his luxurious lifestyle and massive wealth—all of it meant nothing compared to the opportunity for seva. Now he is sitting in an office, and he does not even have an assistant. The beauty of it all is, he doesn't mind; he is content.

4

An Author Par Excellence

'Tolerance is a duty.'
—His Highness Sheikh Zayed bin Sultan Al Nahyan

Then came the opportunity to spend some quality time with Yogi Trivedi, a professor of religion and journalism at Columbia University. Highly articulate and learned would be a mild observation. He is riveting in his speech, having just completed a forty-five-day odyssey writing eighteen hours a day to complete a book on Pramukh Swami's life, called *In Love, At Ease*. Published by Penguin, it is a marvellous read; intimate, deferential, honest and chock-full of details, it is a must-read for a student of religious history just as much as it is for a true believer. Trivedi, according to his publishers, is a former broadcast journalist, communications strategist, classical musician and a scholar of religion and bhakti studies at Columbia University. His time in warzones and monasteries, coupled with his uniquely close relationship with Pramukh

Swami, constitute the foundation for his reflections on the guru's everyday spirituality. Sitting with him endorses in full what his publishers say.

It is the distilled simplicity of his experiences, the depth of his knowledge and his willing surrender to 'the call' that makes for fascinating study. As a biographer extraordinaire for Pramukh Swami, Trivedi's works make for riveting reads. Pramukh Swami, in his lifetime, oversaw the building of more than 1,200 mandirs across India and the world. He initiated over 1,100 sadhus, visited over 17,000 cities, towns and villages across the globe, read and replied to over 750,000 letters and personally counselled over a million people. Answering letters was his trademark and there were probably a lot more he wrote back that were never recorded. The fact that the sanstha is celebrating his centenary with such spontaneous enthusiasm and in such huge numbers, was a testament and a tribute to a life dedicated to the greater good. Do read Trivedi's book on this exceptional life of service, and you will discover several reasons why these swamis see it as a privilege to be followers.

One of the very sensible fiats that Pramukh Swami placed on the order was that to become a swami, one had to get parental permission, regardless of age or education. This mandate assures that the zeal of the aspirant is given the seal of approval. That way, the first step into this new world is taken with honesty and transparency, and there is that certainty that the family has approved. Pramukh Swami believed implicitly that it is not easy to surrender a child, and it was necessary for the parents to be on the same page before the child made such a profound commitment.

Here in the UAE, I was fortunate to have Swami Brahmaviharidas, the senior swami who leads the construction project and is an inspiration to all. His graciousness is absolute, and his presence changes the chemistry of the room. There is an aura about him, a certain assuredness of speech and a depth of knowledge that would be intimidating if it did not come so naturally. He is disarming, but very firm in his views, and spends much of his time talking about the Swaminarayan concept of happy and cheerful collegial togetherness, not in the least demanding.

I ask him teasingly where this glow comes from. It is like an inner light, and they all seem to have it. They probably do not notice it, but it is very much like they have come to terms with an inner peace and found an oasis of tranquility and calm, which reflects in their countenance.

Swami Brahmaviharidas sees the temple in Abu Dhabi as a divine prophecy from high above. He is doing his part to fulfil the wish of his gurus, Pramukh Swami and Mahant Swami. 'We value it,' he says. 'It stands as a testament to harmony and tolerance. And I use the word "tolerance" shorn of the negative connotation that "to tolerate is to endure". On the contrary, tolerance in this context means more than just endurance, it is the willingness to accept and respect differences and diversities. Even if it is a one-way street, it is worth being so with everyone.'

A bit of an aside here would be worthwhile. We have corrupted the word through modern usage to mean enduring something we do not particularly like, be it a person, a trait or a condition. Truth be told, the word was first used in 1510, and its genesis lay in the Latin past participle stem of 'tolerare' (toleratione), which meant 'forbearance, sufferance'. Ironically, it was used to signify permission given by an authority. There is a clear religious element in its history. In 1689, an Act of Parliament in England granted freedom of worship to nonconformists (i.e. dissenting Protestants such as Baptists and Congregationalists). In fact, it was this Act that formed the basis for the Glorious Revolution (1688–89) in England. From the annals of religion to that of culture was a small step. In 1869, the US First Amendment added a rider for 'Tolerance' in the belief that promoting expressive freedoms will make individuals and institutions more open to ideas than they would be otherwise. Today, the UAE with its Ministry of Tolerance, and other nations are cleansing it of that original negative dimension. Caring is tolerance.

5

An Overnight Decision

'The sage goes beyond fear, decay and death. To enter into infinite peace.'

—Prashna Upanishad

In the early days of this assignment, I got to spend quality time with Swami Aksharatitdas, and I value every moment I get with him. His insights are brilliant and spoken with great clarity. Our thrust and riposte in conversations would make for a good talk show, I feel. One day, while working in the United Nations (UN) Office of International Relations in Washington DC, he decided to give Pramukh Swami a call in Ahmedabad and inform him that he wanted to be a swami. At this time, he was doing his major in political science at Northwestern University. It was late at night, nearly midnight, when Pramukh Swami answered the phone and the young, twenty-year-old undergrad said, 'Swami, I want to join the fellowship.'

Pramukh Swami said, 'Have you spoken to your parents? You do that first, then come back to me.'

So, Aksharatit Swami wasted no time. He called his father and said, 'Dad, I want to join the BAPS as a swami.'

His father was quiet for a split second, and then he said, 'Fine, go become one.'

The young man was then advised to change his major to philosophy, which he did, and today, he is the most eloquent spokesperson for this order, or what he calls 'a fellowship of like-minded people doing what they have learnt at the feet of Pramukh Swami and his four predecessors and now with their sixth guru, the much-revered His Holiness Mahant Swami Maharaj.' His Holiness was born in 1933 in Jabalpur. In 1957, the then spiritual leader Yogiji Maharaj joyously gave him the *parshad diksha* and renamed him Vinu Bhagat. For four years, he stayed with Yogiji Maharaj and received spiritual training. He exudes a deep sense of spirituality and stillness. His work speaks for itself; at the age of ninety, he guided the creation of not only this temple in Abu Dhabi, but also the spectacular temples in Robbinsville (USA), Paris (France), Johannesburg (South Africa), Surat (India) and Sydney (Australia).

I regret I was unable to get an audience, but Mahant Swami's emissaries made up for it. Somewhere in the future, I hope it will pan out—and it did.

A story touches me and is an abiding metaphor since it focuses on exactly what Pramukh Swami stood for. Shambu, a young child of six, found his way to Pramukh Swami and requested him to come to his home. Pramukh Swami promised he would. So, the boy waited for the visit, and despite everyone telling him it was not likely, he was certain that Pramukh Swami would come to see him. A fair distance away, Pramukh

Swami was also being dissuaded by his aides on the grounds that it was too cold, there would be much delay and the village of Malav was way off the grid. But the swami said he had given his word, and that word had to be kept; they could not disappoint the child. So they went, canning the schedule for the day, arriving at the child's home much to the shock of the family and neighbours. Shambu was delighted and called all his friends, but he was shy in the beginning and missed the ritual of arti. Swami said, 'Let's do it again,' and asked Shambu to perform the arti. Before leaving, Swami said to him, 'The happiness on your face has driven our tiredness away.'

In that graciousness lies the kernel of Pramukh Swami's lure. People can be made happy with simple deeds. Do them and make them happy.

I look at these very congenial swamis congregating and ribbing, and it is a lot different from what one expects. Many of them educated and living in the UK and USA sound so unlike what one expects swamis in saffron to sound like, and it can get a little unnerving till you get accustomed to the variety of accents. Is it possible that when you give up worldly goods and worldly pleasures and step off that treadmill, there is a space created? That is basic physics. Into that space, you now put compassion, love, duty, commitment, dedication, grace and dignity. And you abide by all these virtues, because there is no other pressure. Does this make sense to you? I am wrestling with these thoughts because it is the first time that I have ever been in such proximity to men of God. For me, that association has so far been limited to sundry pundits performing convenient pujas and cleansing ceremonies at home, ostensibly to ward off the evil eye and make us feel safe—and of course, officiating at weddings and other propitious events. A part of me guiltily felt these rituals were a game for them and as cold as an appointment with the tax collector.

This ambivalence I may have carried with me into the Nagar, but it soon dissipated. It is not easy to write about religion. The armed forces, aviation, politics, even fiction comes easier. Religion is relatively complicated. You either become cynical and slippery clever, or you find yourself stuck in cloying and syrupy superlatives, constantly conscious of causing offence. *What if God is listening and he disapproves?*

It all began in the house of businessman S.M. Rao in Dubai circa 2019. I was with him when Swami Brahmaviharidas and some other swamis came to visit. We were introduced, and on that day, Swami Brahmaviharidas looked me in the eye and said quite categorically, 'We will meet again, that is for certain.'

I didn't think much of it and certainly not about the observation being prophetic. COVID-19 intervened, and two years passed. Even S.M. Rao and I lost touch. Then, one day, while reading about the mandir being built in the capital I wrote an email to Rao, who is also a rather accomplished writer himself, and through him and a very helpful gentleman called Kirti Desai (he keeps a meticulous record of all BAPS activities and feeds me regular updates), I was given the opportunity to meet up again with Swami Brahmaviharidas and Swami Aksharatitdas.

Their green signal to the idea of a book on the mandir, may I say, was expedited by the presence of Ashok Kotecha, another businessman and Chairman of BAPS Hindu Mandir, Abu Dhabi, who encouraged me to give my best. One morning in his office, he selflessly gave me time to share and discuss the enormity of such a project. And we were on. Much of my confidence came directly from him.

I am now in Ahmedabad, scheduled to meet with several senior swamis, and this is unusual because it is not often that one can meet so many of them in such a short span, and I am told that it is, in itself, a very lucky break.

We have a Swaminarayan meal. It is tasty, despite the restrictions against the use of certain ingredients. What is Swaminarayan food? Bhagwan Swaminarayan prescribed that his followers eat only vegetarian food, strictly avoiding meat, fish and eggs. He also prescribed that onions and garlic, which have *tamasic* properties, should not be consumed by his followers. Tamasic foods are those whose consumption, according to yoga, are harmful to both mind and body. There is also a difference between Jain food and this cuisine. Jain food basically places a ban on all root vegetables and some others as well, such as eggplants. Swaminarayan followers do eat root vegetables. Limitations obviously lead to greater inventiveness, and the freshly prepared food can become quite addictive.

Time now to meet some senior swamis. I am a little tense because I am not sure how to conduct myself. All those around me are very comfortable bowing and touching feet. I am not au fait with that very respectful gesture, and I don't particularly want to be seen faking prostration. So, I settle for a bow and a namaskar, which seem to go down well. I am in the presence of Pujya Ishwarcharan Swami, a sadguru swami of BAPS and the global convenor. Well into his eighties, his mind is clear as a bell. He speaks gently and with the acuity of the ages. Speaks about the need for mankind to stop hurting the planet. Tells me that when he dreams, he dreams only of new challenges, for that is the fabric of life . . . to face a challenge and find a solution, everything is cause and effect.

We spend an hour together, and he wants to continue the conversation, but there is a line of people who wish to have his *darshan*, so we respectfully call it a day. He tells me to come again. I then meet Pujya Doctor Swami, also a sadguru swami, and he stuns me a little by emphasizing that I should do a lot more in my life than I am doing, and destiny wants that for me. He blesses me with an abundance of joy and peace, and it is kind of piercing and heartening at the same time because there is no call for it; he does not even know who I am or why I am there. He gives me two pieces of sage advice. Learn to meditate. I facetiously tell him my mind tends to drift off to the cricket score, paying the bills and worrying about unfinished businesses of the day. He just says, 'You can do it.' Then, he tells me to pray. 'But pray from the heart, even if it is for two minutes a day; do it 100 per cent, and see the result. God does listen.' He explains in patient detail that Hindu *shastras* (scriptures) have outlined how a temple of stone must be built, and he says the Abu Dhabi edifice will follow the rules of that ancient architecture and the *shilpashastras*. Yes, indeed, he says it is a miracle ordained by God and his mercy. He believes implicitly that the UAE will be the richer for it as a people who see the future and are a step ahead in their largesse.

We spend more than an hour talking, which kind of surprises his entourage; but we were having such a good time like we were old friends, and he was enjoying it, too—or so I hope.

Later in the day, I sit with Pujya Viveksagar Swami, also a sadguru swami, and it is another delightful experience. He shares his concept of community and the love of the people, all of which supersedes the stone edifice. It is the community that counts. He recalled journalists he knew, especially Khushwant

Singh, and he told anecdotes from way back. Then we talked history and philosophy and the meaning of life and the quest for peace, not just in the world, but the mind. At the end of that meeting, I cannot quite put my finger on it, but I felt as if I have been through a rare experience, something unusual.

6

Awe in Akshardham

'The first gulp from the glass of natural sciences will turn you into
an atheist, but at the bottom of the glass God is waiting for you.'
—*Werner Heisenberg*

By sheer chance, I catch Paramtattva Swami, one of the
leading luminaries in the UK BAPS setup. He is ready to chat.
On the project in Abu Dhabi, he says, 'I would urge you to
do one thing, if you are writing the story of the history of the
Abu Dhabi temple: I would urge you to watch a documentary
series of the making of the Neasden Temple of London. It's
on YouTube. It's got fourteen parts, and each part is about an
hour and a half long. It's a detailed historical narrative with
substantial evidence, phone calls, letters, video interviews,
firsthand witness accounts of how it came up. Struggles.
Planning permission. The choosing of the stone. Why was
Bulgarian limestone used, Italian Carrara marble, granite and
Indian Ambaji marble as well. The whole series is called "First

of Its Kind". You will get a fair idea of what goes into the construction of a temple.

'It was the first-ever traditional Hindu temple outside of India and was inaugurated in 1995. So, you are building an Indian temple thousands of miles away, according to traditional Hindu shastras, using stone from Bulgaria, Italy and other places. To even conceptualize that, bringing all that stone to India, cutting it into pieces, carving it and then shipping it across the ocean and then putting it together again. That is 26,000 pieces, ranging from 150 grams to 50 tonnes. Everything is meticulously done. It is a daunting task.'

He invites me to London to see for myself how well it is going. I might take him up on the offer and fetch up. Just to see the surprise on his face.

When the architects tried to conceive the plans for Abu Dhabi, Swami Brahmaviharidas brought the whole team to London to show them what can be achieved in 5 acres of land. How do you make good use of space, and still provide something beautiful yet functional? That was the aim of the exercise. Most Hindu temples are designed with a rectangular architecture, but the one in Abu Dhabi is distinctively triangular and will be constructed entirely out of stone.

Jet-lagged from his flight from the US is Yoganand Swami. But he is still willing to talk. He is very excited about the Abu Dhabi project and believes it is a high watermark and a breakthrough in inter-religious cooperation, a bridge for the centuries. He echoes the sentiment that this development is a sign of providence at its most beneficent and hopes that there will be more such tangible exchanges between different faiths so that schisms and chasms in understanding are removed or traversed.

And if I was to use one word to forge a common link in these conversations, I would say what comes to mind is visible wisdom. Their years of having been in service to a higher power and dedicating their whole lives to furthering their faith and offering succour to society gives an additional dimension to their demeanour and speech. It is as if they know something we do not, some cosmic secret that they have had a glimpse of, and they cherish.

During the nights of lying in my hotel bed, I contemplate what their mindset might be. There must be something in their DNA that makes them walk away from everything that most of us see as prizes and rewards in life. We do not all have that gene. Even if I was twenty years younger, I might have found it very difficult, even impossible, to get off the gravy train. It needs the pull of a certain celestial command, if that is not being too dramatic. I also sense a certain happy innocence in these senior sadhus, as if shorn of materialism, they have found a delightful childlike glee in celebrating their values and their dedication. I shall say a lot more about these personalities in the second part of this book, because each one brings a distinct vat of knowledge to the table and ladles it out generously.

The icing on the cake has not yet been reached. In New Delhi, by now my friend, guardian and official assistant, Hari Patel, readies me for a visit to the Swaminarayan Akshardham. From a distance, it beckons you and as you get closer, you notice the intense amount of intricate sculpture that makes for the façade. Then, the edifice envelopes you as if in an embrace. The sensation is overwhelming. You fall silent in the face of such beauty and detail and finesse. There must be divinity in these confines; something special, some further dimension. I was once told that in Hinduism, we do not look up to God in the firmament but visit him in his home. Each temple has God in residence, and we seek an audience whenever we enter a house of worship. To that extent, even if there is a soupçon of truth in this interpretation, then God is at home on this cold afternoon in the country's capital. For a moment, it is like everyone else has melted away, and it is just you in communion, your body prickling with pure awe.

My guide tells me that HH Sheikh Abdullah bin Zayed Al Nahyan, UAE's Minister for Foreign Affairs, came and saw and 'concurred' that it was a magnificent shrine and a salute to the Swaminarayan faith.

If you have not been there and you get an opportunity, do not miss it.

It has been a revealing week. I am so much at ease. I will now segue into the second part of the book and trace the path—or rather, several paths—that converged through like-minded people uniting to create this symbol of togetherness: a Hindu temple in Abu Dhabi.

PART TWO

WHEN THE STONES
BEGIN TO SING

7

Through the Looking Glass of Media

'This mandir is like a Cinderella story, a fairy tale more real than real.'

—*Dr S. Jaishankar*

16 August 2015

There is good news and not-so-good news. The USA warns China about secret agents. US President Trump proposes a massive wall on the Mexican border. Syrian forces kill 100 in Damascus airstrikes. US botanists claim that the world's first flower could be the underwater plant *Montsechia Vidalii*. Professional golfer Jason Day wins the 2015 PGA Championship, and Indian Prime Minister Narendra Modi is in his second day's schedule on his visit to the UAE.

Then comes the exceptional news. In a significant development, the UAE decides to allot land for building a temple in Abu Dhabi for the Indian community. Modi writes in the visitors' book, 'I am confident that it will be a symbol of peace, piety, harmony and inclusiveness that are inherent to the faith of Islam. I thank the UAE leadership for this landmark decision.' Later, External Affairs Minister Dr S. Jaishankar would go on record, saying, 'It was Pramukh Swami's dream and prediction, and we are all resolute on it that this temple is made sooner and grander. It is our hope and expectation that we will see BAPS temples in Paris, America, South Africa, Australia, and Thailand. It is "something bigger than a miracle" with two temples—one under construction at Abu Dhabi and another expected in Bahrain—are happening consecutively in the Gulf.'*

Gratitude in great measure to the UAE for saying yes to a long-awaited request and need.

They did not have to say yes. Nobody would have been upset or offended if they hadn't, because no one really believed it would happen anyway. Building a massive Hindu temple in Abu Dhabi was not something that the million-plus expats of the Hindu faith had expected or made any concerted approach to the authorities for.

Over the years, there had been a low-key official attitude to non-Muslims practising their religion. More by design than by fiat, the message was clear: be discreet, do not proselytize, keep the sound low and do not congregate in large numbers.

Those who have lived here since 1972, understood the message and often contributed to the muting through overreach. The hush-hush dimension to satsangs and bhajan gatherings

---

* 'Modi visits Sheikh Zayed Grand mosque in UAE, meets Indian workers', *India Today*, 17 August 2015. Available at: https://www.indiatoday.in/india/delhi/story/modi-visits-sheikh-zayed-grand-mosque-in-uae-meets-indian-workers-288586-2015-08-16.

here was self-generated, as we became victims of our own imagination and duly warned every newcomer to be careful. So long as it wasn't public and noisy, the authorities were tolerant even then. If anything, they were wary of idols being brought into the country, but other accoutrements of faith—if carried through the airport in reasonable amounts for personal use—were ignored.

I recall my bag being opened on a flight from New Delhi. My wife had asked me to bring murtis of Ganesh and Shiva for our little mandir at home. They were about six inches high, and there was also a *lingam* in a copper *diya* to go with it all. I was stressed all through the flight and had clumsily disguised them in wrapping.

In those days, the airport was much smaller, and you did get inspected after you had been reconciled with your luggage. The customs officer asked me to open the bag, then wished to know what it was for, and I told him with dry-mouthed nervousness that it was for the small temple we had at home, and my wife had asked me to bring them along. It was a Pavlovian response, and I began to apologize and dither and was ready to surrender both the items as visions of being carted off to jail for this indiscretion filtered through my mind.

He frowned, then shrugged and told me to put them back in the suitcase and go. I was confused. He was not confiscating them, and that was not something I had been tutored to expect. Our body language sometimes gives us away prematurely. In those early years, we talked to each other about how strict the system was, but no one had ever had a genuine story of anyone getting into huge trouble for bringing small idols or photographs into the country. By that very token, during the eighties, homes of the wealthy had life-size statues of the Hindu pantheon, and they must have come from somewhere.

Newspapers were growing. For us, Obaid Al Tayer, Abdul Rahim, Abdul Latif Galadari and the Taryam brothers were the media moguls. Every now and then, we had a course correction from the offices of Sheikh Hasher, Minister of Information, an immensely courteous personality, always ready to share the reasons behind a decision. Then there was our 'go-to' man, the rock in Abu Dhabi, Ibrahim Al Abid of the National Media Council, who was there for every journalist, whatever the problem, his door open 24/7 in his capacity as an untiring supporter of the fourth estate.

8

A Matter of Trust

'Nothing in life is to be feared. It is only to be understood.'
—*Marie Curie*

I had just been appointed as the editor of *Gulf News*, and at no stage did the owners ever bring up the religion angle during my tenure there. In fact, only once did it come up when we had published by sheer oversight, photographs of an exhibition of artifacts which had pictures of Lord Ganesh and Lord Shiva in the background. An English journalist had not registered what they signified. I received a call from the Ministry of Information to please visit the offices of HH Sheikh Hasher bin Maktoum Al Maktoum, Director General of the Dubai Department of Information.

I was terrified, to say the least, but rushed home, put on a suit and tie, and arrived at the office anteroom, where two very polite gentlemen offered us coffee and dates and biscuits, as my deputy and I sweated bricks. Finally, Sheikh Hasher entered the room and was the epitome of courtesy. He painstakingly and patiently explained why we had been summoned. In brief, such photographs had hurt some sensibilities, and we had to be a little careful. It was a collective admonishment; but that is all, nothing else. I think our relief was amusingly obvious. Not much later, it was Ibrahim Al Abid who put it in perspective. He had already been notified and in a meeting with him in Abu Dhabi, he told me that we need to understand that we are not even 10 per cent of the population, nine out of ten are foreigners. It is a little unnerving, and it is also the reason why they exercise excessive caution. Think of your own countries and the city you live in. What if 90 per cent of the people around you are foreigners? Would you not make security a priority even if it means being 'too' diligent?

We went away from that meeting with some sobriety of thought. Here I am, a Hindu editor in a Muslim nation that is just seventeen years old. My deputy is English and an exponent of Arabic. The news editor is a Sri Lankan Buddhist, and the sports editor is Pakistani. If this was Mumbai, I would be paranoid. These are Emirati people who trust us, and we cannot betray that trust. They have given us their media to run. Indeed, we must be careful.

I share this story with Swami Brahmaviharidas, and he recalls that for sadhus, it was also a fly-below-the-radar time. They would visit for a few days in the 1990s, meet some devotees on the downlow and keep the lowest profile possible. Going to Abu Dhabi was not even on the cards.

'We had this residence which we still have,' he recalls, 'and we would not step out in our robes even for a walk. We had been told to be careful, and we took it very seriously. In fact, in 1997, when Pramukh Swami visited Dubai, we had planned a trip to Abu Dhabi, and so conscious were we of not upsetting anyone or showing ourselves, we went in separate cars, limit of three, each vehicle ten minutes apart so we did not look like a congregation.'

In those days, the prayer meets were held at homes and about twenty-odd like-minded people would meet, keep the microphone muted and literally murmur the bhajans. No one asked us to be so furtive, but by the power of suggestion and self-propelled vigilance from within the ranks, the fear factor stayed intact. So much so that even shoes were not left outside an apartment door because that would be a giveaway that something was going on inside. In retrospect, it was not probably called for to exercise such dramatic vigilance, but that is the way it was.

9

A Handful of Hope

'Yatra vishvam bhavati eka needam. *(Where the world becomes one nest.)*'

—Yajurveda

There was a temple in Bur Dubai in a little lane that became a pilgrimage place and often was so congested, you could not move forward for quite some time. You surreptitiously bought flowers and coconuts and marigold garlands from shops that were holes in the wall, and you hunched your way up the rickety stairs, where an indifferent pundit took your offerings, placed a vermilion *tikka* on your forehead and dispatched you into the U-turn. You could sit for some time while a slightly raucous music system doled out bhajans, but the heat served as a deterrent for a long stay, and the departures were swift.

For smaller gatherings, a few homes had been designated for the gatherings although it was all a bit elitist and obviously not open to the public. Usually at 7 p.m., for an hour, the drawing room at these homes would be shorn of its standard furniture and a few sheets and carpets laid out with a clutch of chairs for the infirm and elderly. There were not many senior citizens in those days because expats from India were relatively young and bringing parents over was a rarity.

Somewhere in the '90s, the concept of inviting Hindu preachers and men of God, rather than godmen, from the mother country increased. They usually stayed at a designated residence and invitations were sent out by phone or word of mouth to have an audience or attend a prayer meeting.

If the authorities knew about it—and one could be pretty certain they did—so far as it was private and not noisy or causing audiovisual disturbance, they let it go.

In contrast to this self-imposed discipline, major festivals did see long queues in Bur Dubai lining up from early afternoon for darshan at the mandir. Diwali, Janmashtami, Shivratri and Ganesh Chaturthi, all saw crowds with a few police in attendance just to keep order and ensure nothing untoward occurred.

On Diwali, for example, homes across the Emirates were lit up with diyas and coloured lights. No one complained, to the best of my knowledge, and firecrackers, though banned, appeared miraculously, and some homes put up actual displays of pyrotechnics.

Every year the 'in' crowd would gravitate to farmhouses for a colour-fest on Holi and the Indian Association would have nearly a thousand revellers doing the *dandiya* dance and flinging fistfuls of coloured powder at one another.

Again, the authorities allowed for these joyful celebrations to continue. Clearly, even in the '80s and '90s, the core of tolerance and togetherness existed and dictated a certain restraint and acceptance of a reality.

As a journalist running newspapers, I will say we were circumspect in our coverage of these annual milestones but by the '90s, photographs of festivals being celebrated in the Emirates began to appear on the local pages. We avoided the overtly religious; so, if it was Vishu or Pongal, the photographs would be of children making *rangoli* designs on the floor. On Diwali, a smiling family lighting a diya would adorn the pages. A long shot of families in the evening queue at the mandir would also suffice. The captions were benign and gentle, and photographs of the Hindu gods were scrupulously avoided.

It is one of the happy ironies that Muslim friends, colleagues and neighbours often joined in these festivities. Emirati sponsors or '*arbaaps*' (abbreviation for Arab fathers or bosses) not only attended, but often had the equivalent of '*bara khaanas*' (feasts) for their non-Muslim staff. Just as much as Hindus and Christians got into the Ramadan mood of abstinence and enjoyed the Eid celebrations, even hosting iftars, their festivals were equally well-attended. I have had Muslim friends who have cheerfully eaten *prasaad* and thought nothing of it.

The religious equanimity and courtesy were a given. The respect was mutual and constant.

A few short years later, there are now several temples and churches and even a synagogue, which can be traced to a camaraderie in the population per se, even as it intensified to reflect over 120 nationalities.

In February 2023, the Abrahamic Family House, an interfaith complex opened in Abu Dhabi. It includes a mosque, a church and a synagogue in one location. The project was announced by the UAE government in 2019 and is aimed at promoting interfaith dialogue, understanding and coexistence.

The complex includes the Imam Al-Tayeb Mosque, named after the Grand Imam of Al-Azhar, Dr Ahmed Al-Tayeb, who is one of the leading figures in Sunni Islam. The mosque can accommodate up to 1,000 worshippers and features modern Islamic architecture.

The church in the complex is named after Saint Francis of Assisi and features modern Christian architecture. It includes a prayer hall that can accommodate up to 700 worshippers.

The synagogue in the complex is named after Rabbi Abraham Cooper, a prominent Jewish leader and activist, and features modern Jewish architecture. It can accommodate up to 500 worshippers.

The Abrahamic Family House is intended to be a platform for interfaith activities and programmes, and it aims to promote values of respect, understanding and peaceful coexistence among people of different faiths. The complex is seen as another symbol of the UAE's commitment to tolerance, inclusivity and diversity.

For decades, the idea of a major edifice on the skyline for a religion that was not Islam, was not on the cards. And yet, the UAE echoed what is so often repeated as a sentiment in the Holy Quran.

The Holy Quran contains several references to religious tolerance and inclusivity. Here are a few examples:

- 'There is no compulsion in religion.' (al-Baqarah 2:256) This verse highlights the importance of freedom of religion and the fact that no one should be forced to follow a particular faith.
- 'To you be your religion, and to me my religion.' (al-Kaafiroon109:6) This verse emphasizes the importance

of respecting other people's beliefs and allowing them to follow their own religion.

We have come a long way in the UAE, and we stand today as a global symbol of the good in mankind. The temple will only add another welcome dimension to this exceptional intent to maintain the integrity of one's religion and one's heritage, while acknowledging all others.

Pramukh Swami's dream or prediction, call it what you may, has come true. His followers marvel at his ability to foretell a development and be unwavering in his belief that an event would occur. It was a prescience that defied explanation and yet gave his persona that aura of divinity, as if he had a direct line to the heavens. But it was not only his dream, prediction or vision that is significant, it is the intent and ethos behind it which impresses me.

That rock-like conviction manifested itself frequently. If something must happen, it has already occurred in the future. Makes sense if you believe time exists as a tangible. When we get a peek into tomorrow, we explain it away as intuition, hunch, a sixth sense, déjà vu, even premonition, a portent or prophecy. Call it the path of destiny.

Whatever way we choose to interpret it, we agree it is a divine decree that ensures what is to happen will happen. At best, for humankind, the most reliable way to predict the future is to create it.

10

Looking into Tomorrow

*'Faith is to believe what you do not see; the reward of this faith is
to see what you believe.'*

—*St Augustine*

So, let's be clear. When Pramukh Swami stood on that dune in
Sharjah and prayed unequivocally that there would one day be a
Hindu temple in the UAE, is it possible that he had the power
to glimpse the future, take a ride on that cosmic plane and make
a prediction based on fact?

One day in 1997, when he was on a visit to the Emirates, he
and a few of the sadhus drove to Sharjah and spent the evening
watching the sun go down behind the sands. A few devotees
had come from England and America as well, who were told
that if sadhus go privately to Abu Dhabi, nobody should
accompany them. We don't want crowds or to do anything
to attract attention or abuse the country's hospitality. Swami
Brahmaviharidas explains, 'Because here there was almost like

a lighthearted litany, we would say, "Swamishri, do you want to go to Abu Dhabi?" and everyone would say no, no, no, no.' Because Abu Dhabi was supposedly very, very strict. So, they went to the dunes of Sharjah. Stand by for further bulletins on this expedition in a moment. For now, let's focus on how the satsang was at that time.

'There would be a small gathering of devotees. One or two Arabs would come at a time to see Swami to get blessings. This was our satsang. At that time, we were so conscious that sadhus never even went out. We didn't go to devotees' homes either.'

His inclusion in the entourage to UAE was fortuitous. There was a big event in Anand, and it was the Holi season. Pramukh Swami summoned Swami Brahmaviharidas and said, 'Are you free?'

'Swamishri, you know you are my guru, you don't even have to ask me if I am free or not.'

'Can you come with me to Dubai? I'm going in a week's time.'

'Such a request is very unusual. Normally, what happens in our institution is when Swamishri travelled abroad, the names of ten accompanying sadhus were always fixed. Two were going to do the katha, one would be translating into English, there would be others who would sing, and things like that. I was like the extra. I didn't need a visa. So, in that way, I came to Dubai in 1997 and now, twenty-six years later, with the grace of my guru and the benevolence of the government, this is my second home.'

Swami Brahmaviharidas tells me, 'The first external sabha in 1997 was done at the embassy. At that time, Prabhu Dayal was the Consul General for India. Such an assembly was so unusual, I still remember the first speech that I gave was "No

Man Is an Island" and that you can't isolate yourself. Then Swamishri would have small meetings with the few devotees who were taking care of the satsang *mandal* in Dubai and Sharjah. Also, we had once gone to a fishermen's village in Al Ain. It was a very small hut-like place where we put up a small murti and started our satsang.

'These were all private gatherings. Nothing systematic, nothing like that. In 1997, there was a Jain social group. Ashok Kotecha and Narendra Jain were a part of that group. They were all Jains and they told Swamishri to go to the deserts of Sharjah. Just to keep them happy, and as Swamishri was relatively frail due to age, initially I went to the desert to see what it would be like. I found it quite interesting, so the next day we went with Swamishri. We were sitting on that dune, and normally, what happens with Pramukh Swami is that he will start saying prayers for everything that is happening. Whether a mandir is being built in the Far East or maybe in Africa or maybe in India, he would pray for it to be completed. Very genuinely, graciously and gently. He would just pray; if there's something adverse happening in the world, he would pray for that to end as well.'

Now, time to take you back to the deserts of Sharjah and the historic nature of the evening's events on 5 April 1997.

Out in the desert that day, Pramukh Swami suddenly started another prayer, expressing hope that the two nations would come closer together. It was a very different prayer.

In the deserts of Sharjah, His Holiness Pramukh Swami Maharaj offered these prayers:

- 'May peace prevail here and everywhere.'
- 'May religions of all countries grow greater love for one another.'

- 'May all countries be free of internal enmity and prejudice, and may they all progress in their own unique way.'
- 'May a mandir be built in Abu Dhabi.'

Swami Brahmaviharidas continues, 'There was a sudden dust storm. Then I said to him, "Do you remember when Yogiji Maharaj [Pramukh Swami Maharaj's guru] had gone to London, he asked everybody to put his chair down [because he was weak, and he could not physically walk] so he could touch the British soil?"

'In much the same fashion, I suggested to Swamishri, even as the sands blew around us, "Why don't you take your sandals off and make contact with the ground." And very prophetically, first he put his toe and then he put his entire foot and said, "May there be a temple in Abu Dhabi!"

'Think of it. We are in Sharjah; we are coming from Dubai, and we are saying that Abu Dhabi is not open to us even for a visit. It's incredible. We didn't know whether to laugh or how to react, because it was such a spiritual moment. Then, he continued with the same idea again, that it will bring countries, cultures and religions closer together. He kept repeating these sentiments.

'Considering going to Abu Dhabi was an comment that we teased him with at night when placing water next to his bed. It was surprising to hear him so fervently say, "May there be a temple in Abu Dhabi!"

In fact, so profound was the statement that Swami Brahmaviharidas and a few others who were with him, were compelled to pick up the grains of sand on which Pramukh Swami had placed his foot and preserve them. They still have them to this day and keep them with due reverence.

'Then we came back, and we still took his prediction very lightly. I'll be very frank; we do not strategize. Our organization is very natural and gentle. There is no compulsion, everything is organic. And everything has the freedom to flourish in its own way. It is a spiritual freeway.

'These premises are reflected in Pramukh Swami's teachings. He always said religion or spirituality has to be as gentle as a breeze. People should love to sit in it and enjoy the zephyr-like sensation. The moment it becomes a wind and a gale force, people start shutting windows.

'That was always his guiding principle. Many religions and religious leaders, once they have many followers, tend to become whirlwinds. People feel afraid, they feel oppressed. They feel compelled to follow because they fear retribution, not the caress of love. Pramukh Swami never forced anyone. Forget about forcing, he gave them more freedom than they could ever imagine. Spiritual comfort was his priority.

'Once, when a devotee asked, "Swamishri, does God listen to our prayers?" Swami said, "Yes." Then the devotee asked, "But when we pray to you, does he hear those prayers?" Swami was eating, and he made a gesture and said, "As you give me, I give to him, whatever you pray to me, I pray to him." Then somebody said, "So, how come all of them are not answered?"

'To that, Swami said very naturally, "It's like the governor. All applications go to him. He will choose to answer those that he wants to answer and those that deserve to be answered. Governors are not compelled to give answers to every query that comes to them."

'Then the devotee said, "But Swamishri, is there a way to jump the queue; is there anything we can give under the table?"

Swami said there is, and I was shocked. Then he said, "Double your faith, and double your devotion. Do greater deeds, and your applications will always be at the forefront," which left all of us introspecting.'

11

Guess Who Is Coming to Tea

'Coincidence is God's way of remaining anonymous.'
—Albert Einstein

Pramukh Swami's ability to 'second guess' providence was best shown during the visit of US President Bill Clinton to Ahmedabad in April 2001. Hear it in exquisite detail from Swami Brahmaviharidas.

'When we heard that the US President was paying a visit to the earthquake-stricken state of Gujarat, we thought it might be a good idea if he came to Swaminarayan Akshardham in Gandhinagar, because that would send out a salutary message to the people suffering from the devastation. I got through to the Secret Service chief of the detail, George Caudill, and I explained for an hour, asking if the president can drop in at Gandhinagar when he is in Ahmedabad and spend a little time at the temple.

'Caudill laughed out loud and said, "Swami, you must be joking. The president's agenda is decided days in advance; there is no way we can do this, forget it."

'Pramukh Swami was in Mumbai, on his way to Dubai that night with an entourage of sadhus. The odds of the president coming were minimal.

'I was determined to try again. I got George on the line and asked him if he could pass on the message to the president and waited for a response, resigned to the fact that there may not be any.

'Then out of the blue, the phone rang on the morning of 4 April, and it was George who got straight to the point. He said, "I have really put my reputation on the line for you, and the president is in the air en route to India at this moment. You will be connected to Air Force One, and you will speak to his schedule coordinator who will put you through to the president. You will get one minute, that is it, just sixty seconds to invite him, and then the line will be cut."

'I said, "I appreciate all your efforts, but I may not be able to speak to the scheduler directly."

'I thought George was going to blow a gasket. "You, you, you . . . are telling me this now? Do you know what it took to arrange this call, and now, you won't talk? I don't believe this. My job is at stake."

'I said, "I understand your concern . . ." "No, you don't, you absolutely do not," he said.

'There was a glacial silence. Then I had a brainwave. I said, you talk to the scheduler, and if the president comes on the line and wishes to talk, I can join in. And that is how it went. The call came through, and Clinton asked if he would be meeting the swami whom he met in Miami. I said, yes, he would, even though Pramukh Swami was hours from boarding the flight to Dubai and had earlier said that he wouldn't be able to come to Ahmedabad. I don't know why I said yes, but perhaps, deep down within me, there was an inner faith that Pramukh Swami would understand.

'Time was running out, and there was no joy coming from George. The only person who seemed unfazed was Pramukh Swami, so much so that he elected to cancel his flight and return to Ahmedabad, giving instructions for us to prepare for the president's visit. I was in a quandary following this development, as things looked bleak. I tried to tell Pramukh Swami that it would be better for him to carry on to Dubai, but he was resolute about changing his plans.

'The day Clinton was supposed to arrive, we just waited. And waited. There was no Secret Service, no advance party, no indication of any security, no one came to sanitize and survey the area.

'Agitated and worried that Pramukh Swami had returned to Ahmedabad and I had failed to deliver, I said I was sorry it had not worked out. I was tense. Pramukh Swami looked me in the eye and said, "He will come, do not worry, he will."

'The conviction in his voice was stirring, but how to tell your guru that the president's movements are choreographed and not spontaneous? That by now the place should have been buzzing with activity. How could he be so sure?

'And then, it happened. A cavalcade roared up. George included. There was a rush of excitement. It was happening. Everyone was galvanized. "Five minutes, young swami and not a minute more," George added that since this was an impromptu presidential call, they were in a rush. It was an unscheduled visit, hence it was come-and-go.'

Swami Brahmaviharidas continues, 'It was around 2 p.m. on 5 April 2001. Security and pilot cars entered Akshardham in Gandhinagar. Before he alighted from his vehicle, the president's security circled the car. Before he stepped out and smiled at everyone, he opened the car door. An empty Diet Coke can fell out. He looked at me and said, "That always embarrasses me," and smilingly, pushed the tin by his heel under the car. That is how natural and charismatic he was, and he told the driver, "Don't move the car." He was introduced to Ishwarcharan Swami, Viveksagar Swami and myself. As he walked towards the main foyer, Mr Clinton was honoured with a red carpet, welcomed by BAPS children showering flowers, amid auspicious traditional Indian music. On seeing Pramukh Swami Maharaj, Bill Clinton was visibly delighted. Swamishri garlanded the president, and he responded with a warm handshake. Clearly, meeting Swamishri in Miami on 4 October 2000 had left a telling impression on him. When we went in, he told Pramukh Swami, "Ever since I met you in Miami, I have always wanted to see you again. Your eyes are full of integrity."

'Then George whispered into my ear, "Five minutes." Pramukh Swami said, "Let's take the president to the Akshardham Mandir." We were at the main entrance, and it takes ten minutes to get to Akshardham, walking, and George had given us five, tops. I asked the president if he would like to see the mandir; he said yes, and then we went. On the way, he asked about the earthquake, even as Pramukh Swami introduced him to all the sadhus, especially the newly initiated from America.

'By now, George was frantically trying to tell me to wind up, but I was with the president, so he could not come close.

Instead, an agitated George sent the sadhus as emissaries. Many sadhus came to me and whispered that George was really upset, but I could not do anything. The president was taking his time. He sat on a sofa and assisted Pramukh Swami to sit next to him, beginning a conversation. He was in such a leisurely and relaxed mood. Looking at Pramukh Swami, he said, "You know everyone in this world thinks that they can get higher by pulling people down, but you do quite the opposite. You help people rise, and you have risen by helping people rise. Look at everybody around you, they look at you with so much love."

'While this conversation was going on, George visibly positioned himself and began making faces, gesturing for me to end the visit. So, in fairness, I said, "Mr President, I believe your time is up."

'He raised his eyebrows and asked, "Why?" I said, "It is because George is making faces at me."

'The president grimaced and said, "Every time I am having a great time, the Secret Service tells me to move on and this once, I am not going to listen to them! So take your time, tell me what else is there to see."

'It is a testament to the magnetism and power of Pramukh Swami that President Clinton went on to visit the exhibitions, watched the presentations and also met the earthquake victims and volunteers. He stayed for ninety minutes, in which time George must have aged ninety years!

'The story does not end here. We were all ecstatic at the end of the visit and its success and basking in the warmth of the aftermath.

'Just as President Clinton was leaving, he asked, "Was the murti inside made of gold? Please tell His Holiness Pramukh Swami that he has a heart of gold."

'Suddenly, while the volunteers were expressing satisfaction, Pramukh Swami asked me, "Did we offer him water?"

'And I said, "Swami, there was no time to offer him water; everything was so rushed."

'Pramukh Swami was so dissatisfied—not angry, but visibly unhappy—and he said, "We should have at least given him water. Call the swamis that were there."

'So I called Vishvavihari Swami who was the head of Akshardham. We were not chastised, but he asked us to write a letter apologizing to Bill Clinton for our lapse in not giving him water to drink.

'I said, "Swami, a presidential letter is normally formal. It would be inappropriate to mention small things. Especially apologizing for not giving water is wholly unnecessary." But he insisted that we be truthful and apologize.

'Later on, we got a message from the White House which appreciated that this letter was unique, as it was the first "thank you" letter that talked about offering water.'

12

Today the World, Tomorrow the Moon

'You cannot believe in God unless you believe in yourself.'
—*Swami Vivekananda*

Pramukh Swami's tryst with the future and what it foretells has become legendary. So often, it happened as he said it. His predecessor, Yogiji Maharaj also had these visions of *que sera sera*. In 1970, Yogiji Maharaj created one of the first Swaminarayan Hindu mandirs in the Western world. At that time, with only a handful of devotees, he declared that in the future 'a mandir with three spires will be built in London'. After Yogiji Maharaj's passing in 1971, Pramukh Swami became the guru. In 1972, when BAPS was still nascent and there were only a handful of swamis, Pramukh Swami envisioned that there would one day be a grand marble mandir in London and that a hundred sadhus would be present for the opening. Traditionally, no one doubts or argues with the spiritual successor of Bhagwan Swaminarayan, but the entourage was bemused. London was so far away and so out of reach that the idea of a major Hindu temple coming up there seemed impossible. As for a hundred swamis fetching up there in the British capital, the very concept was almost laughable.

Fast forward to 1995, the twentieth day of August. A hundred swamis were in Neasden London for the opening of the BAPS Swaminarayan Mandir, described as being Europe's first traditional Hindu temple. It happened as predicted. And it will keep happening.

Where next?

In a flight of fancy, Swami Brahmaviharidas once produced a lunar landscape for Pramukh Swami as a cover for a handcrafted box in which Diwali prasad was placed. It was more a fun thing and done lightheartedly.

He relates the incident, 'Once, I got two of our volunteers, Suresh and Bankim, dressed up as astronauts and sent the prasad box, which was flat and circular. On top, I had put the actual photograph of the moonscape.

'It was 2008 when we did this. I gave the volunteers a small BAPS flag to give to Swamishri. Normally, when a temple is made, a flag is put on top. This was just for fun. Pramukh Swami smilingly said whenever humans settle on the moon, they will need a temple there. Planting the flag exactly in the centre, he said that if it was here, it would be seen from anywhere in the universe.'

Perhaps, it is not a flight of fancy after all. Because in its most recent revival of the lunar expeditions and the Apollo programmes of the 1960s, the Artemis programme intends to re-establish human presence on the moon for the first time since the Apollo 17 mission in 1972. The major components of the programme are the Space Launch System (SLS), Orion spacecraft, Lunar Gateway space station and the commercial Human Landing Systems.

What is delightfully intriguing is that the place chosen for the landing and exploration is right, smack dab where Pramukh Swami had placed the pin. Kush Patel, a devotee, who worked for NASA and now owns the company Relative Dynamics, informed Swami Brahmaviharidas that America is going to resume a manned mission to the moon. The first payload where they will be landing, coincides with the same spot where Pramukh Swami put the flag for the temple. Coincidence or something more celestial? Time will tell, and it will be no surprise because the way it has been going on in the past, surprise is an early casualty . . . anything is possible.

13

The Beginning of the Miracle

'How do we change the world? One act of kindness at a time.'
—Morgan Freeman

In June 2023, twenty-one-year-old Asian-American Max Park solved the Rubik's Cube in 3.13 seconds, setting a new world record. Everything fell into place because he knew where he was going, and so, the destination beckoned with clarity. It is such clarity and such conviction that marks every human aspiration.

There is a great deal to marvel at in this smooth transition from an idea to its fruition, which seems unbelievable, simply miraculous.

Just like a gemologist never throws away his precious stones but simply puts them in their place, we often feel grateful that many a times, moments fall into places without obstructive boulders. Because of that benediction, the impossible enters the realm of the possible and the improbable is suddenly sunlit into the category of probable. While the human element is a vital component in the mix, there is no doubt in our minds that God wills it and brings all parties on to the same page, preempting with great delight the concerns and anxieties and doubts that tend to assail us when we blaze a new trail. It is such conviction and courage which marks the BAPS Hindu Mandir, and it will always be tangible proof that the virtues of togetherness, harmony and peaceful coexistence are still germane to the human experience and not rusting in their own glory.

You might well ask what miracles I speak of, and are they truly miracles or merely pieces of good fortune? Nothing comes from nothing, so there must have been some goodwill in the vat for them to have translated into something concrete.

At the very outset, at the pinnacle of our list of miracles, is the UAE government sanctioning the project to build a Hindu temple in a Muslim country. This is not just a gesture, but what, in the modern context, we call a game-changer. In an era where divisiveness is a currency and suspicion is wielded as a weapon, such a major step generates warmth, love and compassion and so much more closeness and understanding.

This first miracle is not standalone. After the permission came the location for this edifice and out there in this vast desert, under the sand, was a massive stone raft that would make the construction more convenient and robust. Think of it: structural experts said that in a sandy desert, one has to construct hundreds of deep piles for a stable foundation. It is standard practice. However, in this newfound land, exactly where the temple would come, geotechnical surveys found a thick strata of sandstone just a metre under the surface. Not only was it a huge surprise, it was a moment of celebration as Dr Kong Sia Keong, the structural designer from Malaysia, described it, 'The mandir will be as stable as a pigeon on an elephant's back.' What is the probability of discovering such solid foundational stone right beneath the temple, so close to the surface, in a desert of shifting sands? As if it was waiting for this day, knowing the day would come. And it has. Literally a rock-solid premise!

The involvement of the powers that be was not limited to merely signing papers and giving approvals. Here is another miracle in the making. In our wisdom, we had placed the car park in the blueprint design underground and right beneath the temple. When HH Sheikh Abdullah bin Zayed Al Nahyan was told of this plan, he disapproved. 'No, no, no,' he said, 'you cannot have a car park under the temple, it is not right. I will give you more space, don't worry about it.' And so the land granted by the royal family naturally increased, originally from 2.5 acres to 5 acres, then to 13.5 acres, and now with the car park, it extends to 27 acres.

We would not like to spoil the surprises of our list of miracles so patiently and vividly drawn up, except to say some things are destined. The moving finger writes and having writ, moves on . . .

And so do all of us, secure in the knowledge that our temple is not just a house of prayer but a place of learning, of contemplation, of tolerance and of generosity, where the doors are open for anyone, and the human body and human spirit are entwined into a singular entity. Our aim is to create an oasis of peace and tranquility, for grand thought to flourish and the arts and sciences to thrive. So that when history is written and a thousand years from today, the edifice endures, it will be a symbol of what can be achieved when our hearts and minds are one.

Our miracles are indeed a tribute to this great country, its enlightened rulers, and their long-distance vision of a world of oneness.

* * *

We are in New Delhi on a cold winter January morning and are welcomed with warmth from the former Ambassador of India to UAE, Navdeep Suri, sipping *kadak* tea. He was instrumental as a bridge between government agencies and BAPS representatives. I will hand over the pen to him now, for his is a story that puts things into perspective. He starts at the very beginning, which is a very good place to start.

'I really think that my involvement in the construction of the first Hindu temple in Abu Dhabi was one of the highlights of my tenure in the UAE. It started even before I arrived in Abu Dhabi, after I had moved from Australia. I was in Delhi for a week prior to taking charge in Abu Dhabi. I called on the late Foreign Minister Sushma Swaraj in her office to get a briefing on what were the priorities and so on. She said, "Look, Navdeep, I know that Dr Jaishankar will brief you, as is right. But amongst the things I really want you to take up is this matter of the temple. A trusted organization called BAPS is building the temple. Please support them. It is of utmost importance. A prime ministerial commitment."

'Within, I think, three or four days of my arrival in Abu Dhabi, I invited a delegation from BAPS. It was my first meeting with Swami Brahmaviharidas, and he came along with four or five of the key members of the temple committee.

'They said to me that they needed to brief me on where they were in the proceedings. There were some issues with the land that'd been allocated, and they needed to address them and then speed up the whole process.

'While the UAE government was looking for alternative sites to increase the land size, it was taking a little longer and the temple committee was unclear on the official process.

'The government proposed to give us more land, I think 10 acres or more, at the new site. Then we looked at the map, and we said this was wonderful. It was almost equidistant from Dubai and Abu Dhabi, and so it's easily accessible to all communities; it was a blessing in disguise.

'My principal port of call was the Ministry of Foreign Affairs and International Cooperation during these initial negotiations.

'Within that, because this was something that had been agreed at the highest levels, a lot of the direction was coming from the office of His Highness Sheikh Abdullah as the foreign minister and in fact, he designated his chief of staff, Mohammed Al Khaja, as the point person to help us out. So, I used to go to Mohammed Al Khaja to resolve any issues. He was a great help and support, and much was done through his good offices.

'There were challenges because building a temple was completely new for the government books. Right from obtaining permissions, enabling clauses, notifications, exemptions and regular approvals. The fact that BAPS was a very upright, transparent and truthful organization generated huge trust and respect. While all government procedures were followed, they were done with a great amount of ease and happiness. I had the great privilege of being a part of this process.'

Navdeep offers some dainty sweets and asks if we want another round of tea. We demur, and he skates into the next developments.

14

Stepping Stones to Success

'Just as a candle cannot burn without fire, men cannot live without a spiritual life.'

—*Gautam Buddha*

Navdeep is clear about his assessment. 'I have to say from the BAPS side, there was this real intent that everything must be above board. They were willing to take more time but wanted everything properly in place. We went along that road for a fair bit. I think much after I arrived in Abu Dhabi in December 2016, and through 2017, we spent a lot of time sorting out the fundamentals and getting our ducks in a row. This included finally getting the title of the land for the temple, and we got support from HH Sheikh Abdullah throughout this process. And that made things so much easier.

'Towards the end of 2017, the prime minister had accepted an invitation from HH Sheikh Mohammed bin Zayed to come as the guest of honour at the World Government Summit in February 2018.

'As part of the programme, we agreed that he would do a symbolic launch of the temple. We discussed in lengthy sessions whether it would be virtual or on-site. Eventually, we agreed that a replica of the temple would be launched during the big event at the Dubai Opera. So, we got down to work.

'Swamiji said that we must create a replica that the prime minister can unveil. But what kind of temple was it going to be? I said, "What do you mean by that?"

'He said, "Ambassador, let me put this very simply. On the one side, you can have a traditional stone temple in all its glory with sculptures and classical architecture, or you have something like a regular rectangular building within which a non-traditional house of worship can function, which is low-key and less visible."

'At this juncture, I had no idea what the government would say about this. Swami Brahmaviharidas gave me two designs in a book and said, "Here are the two options." I said, "Alright, leave it with me," and I took time from the foreign minister, though first, I went to see Mohammed Al Khaja and I said, "Look, my friend, this is a little bit urgent because based on what you say, the decision about what is going to be unveiled will be taken." He said, "Leave it with me." What an exceptional man.

'I had also used that opportunity to happy advantage. India's Republic Day was approaching, so I used the opportunity to request Mohammed Al Khaja if we could have HH Sheikh Abdullah grace the occasion as the chief guest and the invitation to honour us was accepted by the foreign minister. It was a great feeling.

'Towards the end of the event, as I was escorting Mohammed Al Khaja to the back, he pulled me aside for a minute and said, "I have some good news for you. I discussed about your temple style with HH Sheikh Mohammed, and he was very clear. We agreed to have a temple in Abu Dhabi, so it should look like a true traditional temple."

'That was the end of the story. So, next morning, with great delight, I conveyed this to Swami Brahmaviharidas, and very quickly, they got the model together in time, and it is that which was unveiled by the Prime Minister of India.'

Navdeep continued, 'I also put in a request asking if we could arrange a call. Could we also invite the swamis to the meeting and collectively call on HH Sheikh Mohammed? That happened on 10 February, if I'm not mistaken.

'There was this big reception that the President of UAE, then the Crown Prince, held in the Presidential Palace. It was a pleasure for me, and you could even say a very satisfying optic to see Swamiji with members of the temple committee present a book which outlined the vision for the temple to HH Sheikh Mohammed in the presence of our prime minister. For me, it was an unusually memorable moment.

'The next major milestone in this epic saga was HH Sheikh Abdullah's very substantive visit to India. He spent five or six days here and visited different places. I worked out a schedule for HH Sheikh Abdullah. In that programme, particularly the time that he was to be in Delhi, I recommended that he visit Humayun's Tomb and Swaminarayan Akshardham. The suggestion was accepted.

'He did visit Akshardham, and I think initially there were some reservations about his making it since his programme was very tight. Finally, it was decided he would come for half an hour.

'Can I just say he was so impressed by the magnificence of the temple and the way the whole story was narrated to him about the temple. HH Sheikh Abdullah not only spent about two hours visiting the temple, but then stayed back for the laser and water show as well. That is what happens frequently with VIP visitors; they just want to stay and absorb the atmosphere. It washes over them.

'I think that perhaps more than anything else, he really got to see the spirit behind the temple, and this strengthened his resolve to encourage the project back home even more.

'Everybody was onboard from the leadership and what that meant was that after that, if it was something that the ministry of community development dealt with or somebody else dealt with, things moved much more quickly. And our lightning rod Mohammed Al Khaja was always at hand to expedite matters.

'We were still debating some issues, especially about land for parking. We thought, "Are we going to make it underground?" By that time, we had made a fair bit of progress, so Swamiji said it would be good to update HH Sheikh Abdullah on where we were.

'Mohammed arranged for us to meet HH Sheikh Abdullah at his private residence in Abu Dhabi, and Swamiji and I drove there. It was very informal, warm and beyond cordial, and I recall we spent a fair bit of time with him. During that meeting, the issue of parking came up. We said it's going to take us a while because the soil is very hard; it is very rocky under the sand, and we have to dig deep into the basement for creating a parking space.

'I remember HH Sheikh Abdullah saying, "Do you really want to do that? It's not just a question of cost, but it's also a question of safety to have that many cars in the basement on your special days."

'The logic of his words was undeniable, but we seemed to have no choice. But he did.

'"Why don't we look at more land?" he said, much to our amazement. More land. And yes, it happened. From that little conversation, the mission doubled in space. Within a couple of weeks, we were given an additional 13.5 acres. That is the parking area now.

'It had twin advantages. We got additional land for our overground parking, but it also reduced the cost of an underground lot substantially. As we were later to discover, because that ground was so hard, you know it made the foundation much stronger for the temple. Somebody up there loves us.

'Let me get a little personal here. With this background and the buildup, the biggest day after that was to join in for the *shilanyas*, the laying of the foundation stone of the temple. To be there to participate in the ceremony and really be part of what you might say history being created in a different land . . .

'When I look back, I would say that there are three or four key drivers that posterity should keep in mind. One, of course, is that the initiative for the temple came from the prime minister, and also the role that Mrs Sushma Swaraj played in monitoring and keeping things on track in those early days.

'The second is really both the degree of organization and the sophistication with which BAPS took this process forward. I really can't think of any other religious organization that is so well-organized or which favours the latest logical trends. Often with the nuts and bolts of construction, you need an army of volunteers that are willing to more than chip into the process, and BAPS has them in plenty.

'The third is all the members of the community, who generously agreed to put money into the temple. Again, it was amazing for me to see firsthand how lay members of the community and the sadhus who were involved in it would step forward every time something was being planned. There was no hesitation.

'Last and not the least—and I do want to emphasize this—I think we must remember the crucial role played by the royal family of Abu Dhabi. I keep saying in my various public engagements and addresses of how our relationship with UAE has been transformed and certainly, the temple is a symbol of that. And while it's nice to pat ourselves on the back for the work that we might have done, make no mistake—it is primarily an indication of how much UAE has changed as a society. Change that is driven by the leadership from the top. It is mature, truly visionary and far-thinking.

'Abu Dhabi was always a conservative society. For Abu Dhabi to change within such a short span of time and to say that we will have this grand temple, was amazing. It was done with incredible grace, incredible generosity. That one line, "It should look like a temple," showed the mindset of the leadership.

'I subsequently had occasion to discuss this with a couple of other members of the royal family that I won't name. I was expressing my appreciation for this approach of the leadership. And one of them said, "Ambassador, when I go overseas to Europe or somewhere else and I am in my hotel, I hear the *azan* coming from a mosque in the neighbourhood; I like it. But then I have the responsibility to come back and tell my people if I can hear the azan in Paris or London, what's wrong with me hearing temple bells in my country?" It is exactly this sort of thought process that underscores great governance.

'I think, again, it's an indication of how sensible and enlightened leadership can drive change in society. The clarity they had while pursuing this enterprise is a telling part of the bigger picture of the change in the UAE, now reflected in the Abraham Accords, and in the Abrahamic Family House that's come up in Abu Dhabi, with a mosque, church and synagogue in the same premises. All three buildings are the same in terms of size, dimensions and so on. It's really a very visual way of bringing out equality of faiths.

'You know you can see other examples, but you know having somebody such as HH Sheikh Nahyan as the Minister of Tolerance is a major force. He was a key driver at multiple places. I really regard HH Sheikh Nahyan as a very dear friend, if that is not presumptuous. He was the one to whom I could go informally and chat. And you know his support was also very salutary [because he's such a popular figure in the UAE]. He always found time to come to our events. Again, it is a very public way of saying, "This is endorsed by the royal family at the highest levels." These are messages that trickle down the system and work wonders.'

Navdeep concluded, 'Since I am being "interrogated", let me say this. I really treat Swami Brahmaviharidas with a huge amount of respect. He's an extraordinarily capable person, but he's also become a friend over the last three or four years. I keep pointing out that isn't it weird I'm agnostic, bordering on atheism, and yet I'm involved in this? For me, it also became one of my key deliverables during my tenure in UAE. So, if I were to say name three milestones of my stint, I could say the temple, work with the Abu Dhabi investment authority to attract major investments into India, the work with Abu Dhabi National Oil Company (ADNOC) to get our first oil concession and our first strategic petroleum reserves. For me, those are some of the real highlights, and the temple is part of that, most certainly.'

15

Did the Wrong Set Things Right?

'Being truthful is being peaceful.'
—His Holiness Pramukh Swami Maharaj

Never apologize for something you believe in. It could be a career, a commitment, even an act of kindness or courage. Perhaps your faith. Wear them all on your sleeve.

It is this sentiment that marks the first beginnings of the BAPS Hindu Mandir's rising in Abu Dhabi. Its genesis is always amazingly surprising. You would think it would be something profound, a green baize table with bottled water and a conclave of VIPs seriously debating the pros and cons as padded stewards serve refreshments.

In real life, it started with an honest mistake that makes for a delightfully disarming story.

In the '90s, when the sadhus would visit the UAE, mostly Dubai, they would float from one residence to another with the singular aim of protecting the continuation of the satsang.

For thirty-two years, the temple premises where they held discourses were the size of a postage stamp, enough to fit about thirty people in a pinch.

Larger premises were offered by devotees, but like creatures of habit, no one wanted to make the move. There was a whole slew of excuses made to stay where they were. The new place might cause inconvenience to the neighbours, the smell of cooking might annoy them, it's difficult to reach, what if anyone objects; all conveniently 'good' reasons to stay the shift.

It was in 2013 that there was a small villa offered in the Al Satwa area of Dubai. Rohit Patel and Ghanshyam Pagarani, both successful businessmen, who were great supporters of BAPS, said we will share the rent, let's take it. Then again, the same set of excuses were trotted out and the reluctance was tangible. It was Swami Brahmaviharidas who said there's no harm in going and seeing it before deciding.

And that is how this saga begins. The place was taken, and people came in for the sessions, but it was all kept low-profile.

A few months into using this villa, organizers decided to remove a partition between two rooms and enlarge the space where people could sit more comfortably. However, little did they realize that they could not make any alterations within the villa without prior permission.

The authorities appeared and explained the issue. Since Pramukh Swami always believed in honesty above everything else and respected the smallest of laws of the land, Swami Brahmaviharidas adopted the most truthful and transparent approach.

In fairness, devotees had tried to fill in the official forms for the Community Development Authority (CDA) and observe the formalities, but were overwhelmed by their

5 April 1997. Deserts of Sharjah, UAE.
Pramukh Swami praying, 'May a temple in Abu Dhabi
bring greater peace and global harmony.'

9 February 2018. BAPS Hindu Mandir Site, Abu Dhabi.
Rohitbhai Patel, a founder member of BAPS Satsang in the UAE,
standing on the mandir land with Swami Brahmaviharidas, recalling
the 1997 prayer made by Pramukh Swami.

10 February 2018. Qasr Al Watan, the Presidential Palace, Abu Dhabi. Swami Ishwarcharandas and Swami Brahmaviharidas present two temple concepts to His Highness Sheikh Mohamed bin Zayed Al Nahyan and Prime Minister Shri Narendra Modi. His Highness approves the traditional stone temple.

11 February 2018. Dubai Opera, UAE. The Prime Minister of India Shri Narendra Modi unveils the model of the BAPS Hindu Mandir, Abu Dhabi.

26 June 2018. Swaminarayan Akshardham, New Delhi.
His Highness Sheikh Abdullah bin Zayed Al Nahyan in dialogue
with Swami Brahmaviharidas, admiring the architectural grandeur
of Swaminarayan Akshardham, New Delhi.

12 October 2020. Deserts of Al Ain, UAE.
His Highness Sheikh Abdullah bin Zayed Al Nahyan appreciates the
selfless global services of BAPS Hindu Mandir during the COVID-19
pandemic and the mandir's continued progress despite challenges.

19 August 2018. Atladara, Gujarat, India.
HH Mahant Swami Maharaj guides the designs for the
BAPS Hindu Mandir, Abu Dhabi.

20 April 2019. BAPS Hindu Mandir Site, Abu Dhabi.
His Holiness Mahant Swami Maharaj and members of the UAE
leadership place the first brick for the mandir during the foundation
stone-laying ceremony.

21 April 2019. Abu Dhabi, UAE.
His Excellency Sheikh Nahyan Mubarak Al Nahyan hosts
HH Mahant Swami Maharaj in his Royal Majlis.

21 April 2019. Grand Mosque, Abu Dhabi.
HE Sheikh Nahyan Mubarak Al Nahyan guides HH Mahant Swami
Maharaj hand in hand through the Sheikh Zayed Grand Mosque with
great love, friendliness and respect.

8 January 2023. Ahmedabad, Gujarat, India.
An evening at the month-long Pramukh Swami Maharaj birth centenary celebrations (PSM100), where over 12 million gathered from around the world to celebrate the life of Pramukh Swami.

18 January 2023. Ahmedabad, Gujarat, India.
Over 80,000 BAPS volunteers gather for an appreciation ceremony upon the conclusion of PSM100.

25 May 2023. BAPS Hindu Mandir, Abu Dhabi.
Swami Brahmaviharidas addresses an international delegation of
ambassadors from over thirty nations, sharing the universal message
of the BAPS Hindu Mandir.

25 May 2023. BAPS Hindu Mandir Site, Abu Dhabi.
Ambassadors are given a tour of the mandir to appreciate its beautiful
architecture and ancient construction techniques.

1 January 2024. BAPS Hindu Mandir, Abu Dhabi.
On the exterior of the mandir, fourteen value tales from ancient
civilizations teach timeless lessons. In this tale from the ancient Mayan
civilization, two Aztec warriors learn the value of friendship and harmony.

21 December 2023. BAPS Hindu Mandir, Abu Dhabi.
Exquisite carvings depicting the Ramayana immortalize the
values of devotion and righteousness.

5 December 2023. BAPS Hindu Mandir, Abu Dhabi.
The mandir also features birds and animals from the UAE,
such as the Arabian oryx, falcon and camel.

21 December 2023. BAPS Hindu Mandir, Abu Dhabi.
Artisans expertly place one of the 30,000 carved stones—ranging
in weight from under 1 kilogram to over 6 tonnes—layer by layer
like a giant 3D jigsaw puzzle.

15 September 2022. BAPS Hindu Mandir Site, Abu Dhabi.
Over 70,000 individuals from around the world lent a hand to harmony
by placing a brick during the mandir's construction.

14 January 2024. BAPS Hindu Mandir, Abu Dhabi.
The Dome of Harmony features the five foundational elements:
earth, water, fire, air and space.

14 January 2024. BAPS Hindu Mandir, Abu Dhabi.
Known as the 'Pillar of Pillars', a singular marble block transformed into
a stunning array of 1,400 pillars by twelve artisans in one year.

13 January 2024. BAPS Hindu Mandir, Abu Dhabi.
Artisans and volunteers join in to complete the mandir in the
final stages of its construction.

15 January 2024. BAPS Hindu Mandir, Abu Dhabi.
The seven spires of the mandir represent the seven emirates of the UAE.

8 October 2023. Robbinsville, New Jersey, USA.
BAPS Swaminarayan Akshardham, created by His Holiness
Mahant Swami Maharaj, is one of the world's largest Hindu mandirs.
Around 12,500 volunteers helped assemble this landmark of
Hindu culture, art and architecture.

14 Frbrurary 2024. BAPS Hindu Mandir, Abu Dhabi.
Bhagwan Swaminarayan and Aksharbrahma Gunatitanand Swami,
his first spiritual successor.

'In the joy of others lies our own.'
His Holiness Pramukh Swami Maharaj, the inspirer.

'More than stones or bricks, this mandir
will be an abode of love, peace and harmony.'
His Holiness Mahant Swami Maharaj, the creator.

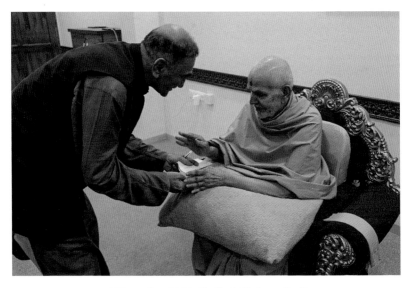

9 December 2023. Nadiad, Gujarat, India.
The author meeting His Holiness Mahant Swami Maharaj.

"This mandir is like a lotus blossoming in the desert"
HH Mahant Swami Maharaj

11 February 2024. BAPS Hindu Mandir, Abu Dhabi.
Hundreds of supporters, devotees, and well-wishers gather for the inaugural
Mahayagna for harmony, a momentous occasion marking the first of its
kind in the history of the Middle East.

14 February 2024. BAPS Hindu Mandir, Abu Dhabi.
HH Mahant Swami Maharaj performs the Murti Pratishtha, infusing divinity into the murtis of Swaminarayan Bhagwan and Aksharbrahma Gunatitanand Swami.

'For thousands of years, Bharatvarsh and humanity will be grateful for what you have done. This is an amazing achievement'
Prime Minister of India, Shri Narendra Modi

'Today marks the beginning of something very special. This temple will serve both as a place of worship and as a place that will strengthen bonds for the entire community' HE Sheikh Nahyan Mubarak Al Nahyan, Minister of Tolerance and Coexistence

14 February 2024. BAPS Hindu Mandir, Abu Dhabi
HH Mahant Swami Maharaj launches the book
A Millennial Moment with Prime Minister Narendra Modi

23 February 2024. BAPS Hindu Mandir, Abu Dhabi
HH Mahant Swami Maharaj appreciates the intricacy
of the carvings and the pillars of the mandir

1 March 2024. BAPS Hindu Mandir, Abu Dhabi
A sea of lamps; Devotees gather in thousands at the
Swaminarayan Ghat to partake in the Ganga Arti

complexities. Since these visits had never seen any interaction between the sadhus and the local population, there was not a single Emirati with whom they were familiar. So, there was no one they could approach and ask for guidance. All these years, it was just congregating at the home of businessman and hotelier Lakho R. Lulla or some other place such as the Ambassador Hotel in Bur Dubai. Once, they had a session at the Crown Plaza following the Bhuj earthquake as a community support group, but not much else. The bunny-hopping between homes and apartments led to a certain seclusion from the locals and suddenly, there was this situation rising like a massif in front of them. After nearly fifteen years of being low-profile and not shaking the tree here, they were in a storm. They knew no official, and there was no recourse to the royals. But they had heard of the *majlis* option, where anyone could fetch up and get his day in court with a high-profile dignitary. It was decided that Swami Brahmaviharidas would attend the majlis of HH Sheikh Nahyan Mabarak Al Nahyan, Minister of Culture. Maybe he would grant them a hearing. Good things had been said about him, so it was worth giving it a try.

By his own confession, Swami Brahmaviharidas was nervous about this visit, but took heart from the teachings of his mentor, Pramukh Swami. He says, 'Pramukh Swami Maharaj had taught us to not shy away from challenges and had encouraged us to express true emotions without any arrogance. In 1981, when I had been freshly initiated as a monk, I had written a letter to Pramukh Swami in English. I had come from England and was very open-minded. I wrote that if I find anything fanatic in this religious order, I will leave. Imagine the large-heartedness of Pramukh Swami. He was a religious leader par excellence, globally respected, and I was just an unknown novice who was coming into the order; I wrote him this in the very first days. And yet, the universality and humility of Pramukh Swami was more open than my mind and heart put together. In the decades to come, every time he would meet me, he would ask if I was fine and if things were okay; an oblique reference to my immature rawness of that one day. For forty years! Such is the freedom he gave. You can allow your heart to beat to the rhythm of your own heart. So far as it is for the greater good, he never controlled the rhythm of your heart, which was the beauty of his spirituality.'

And it is this sense of confidence that propelled Swami Brahmaviharidas towards the majlis, even though there was trepidation that it could go very wrong.

As the journey continued, he found more comfort in his master's teachings.

'Pramukh Swami Maharaj always taught me that when you begin the day, you must be attached to the task ahead of you. Own it. Give it all you have as if there is no one else around to help. But when you end the day and complete the task, you must become detached from its success or failure. Thank God and everyone for making it happen. Do not own the rewards. Share them with all. Hence, every night, when Pramukh Swami went to bed he was always happy, with innocent laughter. Sometimes, there would be a huge gale of laughter. If things had gone right, God was thanked. If things had gone wrong, again God was thanked, as at the end of the day, it is his wish that prevails throughout the day. Without misery or malice, it was just genuine joy and laughter to close the day, a deep cleansing of the body and soul, often triggered by human stories of our daily deeds.'

So, driving to the majlis, his mind was whirring like a clockwork toy. The Sheikh was not there yet, but sitting among the few guests, in his simple orange attire, Swami Brahmaviharidas stood out. The others were curious to see him in their midst, but not the least bit hostile, which offered Swami some relief. In fact, they are quite friendly. And very curious.

'Tell us,' says one, 'why are your clothes orange?'

Swami is silent for a moment and then he gives an eloquent answer. 'We are Hindus and when we pass away, we are not buried, we are cremated, and the colour of the fire that consumes our body is either yellow, orange or red. This orange colour is a constant reminder that we are dying every day and every minute; so do as much good as you can, to as many people as you can, in as many ways as you can, for as long as you can.'

There is a respectful silence, and they nod at the wisdom inherent in the explanation. It is a bit stunning in its unexpectedness. At that point, HH Sheikh Nahyan arrives and there is a flurry of activity. As the congregation settles down, Swami recalls, 'I am clearly the odd one out and a second question is flung at me; this one more complex, almost a challenge.'

'Can you tell us who is the founder of Hinduism, and what is the main book of Hinduism?'

'This is a complex question. I try to soften it by saying it might need a great deal of time. They collectively say, "Oh no worries, we have time, go on, speak."' Swami then said to them, 'Every question is conditioned by history, culture and nurture. In an era of wars, victories and conquests are glorified. In times of trade, success and wealth are worshipped. In a mighty multinational corporation, conversations are centred around growth and competition, while in a farming society, talks will revolve around crops and weather. Similarly, for religious people who are used to a religion that has a single founder and a single book, this question is valid.

'Come East, and it gets a little more dynamic; Hinduism is more fluid.' By now, Swami had the riveted attention of the majlis. He asked, 'Do you or do you not believe that religion is a stream of knowledge? Just as a flowing river or a stream nourishes its shores with gardens, flowers and fruits, religions have been nourishing and enriching people with beautiful values. Each genuine religion in its own way has been spiritually transforming society for many centuries. Science, too, is a stream of knowledge which, with all its wondrous inventions and grand technologies, has been enriching and transforming society. The cars, the planes, the gadgets and the comforts—all have emerged from books of science. Now tell me, who is the founder of science, and what is the main book of science? Would you single out Aryabhata, Sushruta, Aristotle, Archimedes, Newton, Galileo, Edison, Marie Curie, Einstein, Heisenberg, or Hawking as the founder of science? Or would you identify *The Origin of Species*, *Principia Mathematica*, *General Theory of Relativity* or any one work as the main book of science? Every scientist has contributed to the river of science. Science has no one single founder and no one book. Every book of discovery or theory has added to the flow of science. Science is beyond any one individual or any one discovery.'

There was pin-drop silence.

Swami continued to address what was now a rapt audience, 'Because science has become so vast, it is almost timeless. It began when early man picked up two stones and made the first spark, and it is now the same river sending man into deep space. What an incredible journey which continues to continue.

Hinduism is like spiritual science, a constant flow of knowledge. It began before the beginning of man, and it will continue after man; and that is why there is no single founder, no single book. Every true Hindu leader and every Hindu scripture contributes to the eternal flow of Hinduism known as 'Sanatan Dharma'— the timeless eternal religion, without beginning or end.'

There is a quietness in the majlis; there is a canopy of contemplation, and it is like they were absorbing the answer and were quite comfortable with its underpinning logic.

Then HH Sheikh Nahyan gracefully turned to Swami and asked the purpose of his visit. Swami goes into an elaborate explanation about how the partition in the small villa in Dubai was removed unknowingly and innocently and expressed his profound regret for this honest mistake.

The truth and honesty in the voice of Swami Brahmaviharidas touched the Sheikh, who smiled and comforted him, 'You are transparent, truthful and well-meaning, so do not worry. The officials in Dubai will understand the purity of your purpose.'

This moment gave Swami a great surge of confidence. The rulers were kind, compassionate and understanding, very fair and just leaders. Truth be told, that was the first step taken towards the temple becoming a reality. The first stepping stone on a long path.

Swami left the majlis feeling a sense of gratitude and relief. Little did he know that his path and the path of HH Sheikh Nahyan would cross on numerous occasions, and they would hold each other in great and mutual esteem.

And with God's grace, the officials understood and appreciated the message of harmony Swami Brahmaviharidas was spreading. Months later, HH Sheikh Nahyan personally encouraged Swami to write a letter to the Crown Prince of

Abu Dhabi HH Sheikh Mohammed bin Zayed Al Nahyan
for a piece of land to build a temple. Perhaps, in hindsight,
everything just came together to make things right. Even the
innocent mistake in the villa became the reason for the meeting
in the majlis. In life, doing the right thing at the right time, at
the right place, for the right reason, in the right way, is perhaps
God-guided.

And when one is inspired by God, one rises beyond one's
own achievements and attainments.

Yes, a temple in Abu Dhabi was a historic and great
achievement, but Pramukh Swami's teachings went beyond the
arena of achievements.

Every little time spent with him was precious; like little
children gathering seashells on a beach, spiritual seekers
collected nuggets of knowledge and wisdom. One such moment
of inspiration occurred years ago when Pramukh Swami was
younger and in better health. In the early '90s, in New Delhi,
Swami Brahmaviharidas once entered Pramukh Swami's room
to discover several sheets of paper on a table. 'What is this?' he
asked.

'Not for you,' replied Pramukh Swami, 'Leave them
alone.'

'Well, Swami,' Swami Brahmaviharidas said in jest, 'it isn't
for you either; it is in English.'

Turns out, it was a list of over 300 BAPS Swaminarayan
temples constructed worldwide by Pramukh Swami which the
Guinness World Records had prepared. Because Pramukh Swami
did not read or write in English, Swami Brahmaviharidas said,
'Swamishri, in which year did you make the temple in Mahudha
and the one in Mumbai? What about the ones in Africa and the
US?' Pramukh Swami did not recall any of them, shrugged and

dismissed it as inconsequential. But then, he said something striking. Life-changing.

'Those who make temples do not make lists. Those who make lists do not make temples.'

For Swami Brahmaviharidas, it was a defining moment, one he treasures for its relevance. Once again, he had mistakenly picked up the wrong papers and discovered lifelong answers. We must do what we must do and not keep records of our successes or failures. We must move on because life goes on.

16

Lessons to Be Learnt

'No legacy is so rich as honesty.'

—William Shakespeare

The time has come, the walrus said, to talk of many things: Of shoes . . . and ships . . . and sealing wax . . . Of cabbages . . . and kings . . . and wild imaginings. There you are then; we have successfully paraphrased Lewis Caroll and the theme from *Love Story*. It was a time to give love and a time for more than wild imagining.

We speak of the art and science of religion. Art because it involves imagination and an open mind, which is needed for expression to go into free-fall. Science, because it has fact as its cornerstone and just because like an iceberg, we do not know its entire extent does not mean it is fiction. Both the skeins of art and science rope together to create the harness of true faith.

'Dharma' is the first word mentioned in the *Bhagavad Gita*.

Many get confused by this word and broadly think of it as religion. It refers to the Hindu way of life.

The word 'dharma' comes from the Sanskrit verb '*dhri*'. '*Dhri dharayati iti dharma.*' That which sustains, upholds, is dharma. Dharma is the essence of one's identity and existence. That which makes a human, human. Hence, dharma does not translate to just religion. It is more. It also means righteousness, duty towards oneself, duty towards society and duty towards God. The *Bhagavad Gita* emphasizes that every righteous thought, word and deed is personal dharma. Perfection in action is dharma, while detachment from desires and action is also dharma. While overcoming anger, jealousy and ego is dharma, complete surrender to and faith in God is also dharma.

Pramukh Swami understood this and that is why he never judged, just made corrections to the course. In modern terms, ask any pilot and he will tell you that flying is only about minor adjustments along the way. So is our relationship with God. He has given us a route map, and it is up to us to follow it, but we stray to use our 'common sense' and fail to make these vital corrections. In attitude, in altitude, in direction and definitely in handling the controls to ensure your passengers who depend on you, remain comfortable. The swamis look at it in such a way, too. They guide you to your destination because that is the promise.

Saturday, 13 August 2016, will always be a day of quiet despair, as the body of Pramukh Swami breathed its last and his soul departed. More than 2 million faithful converged from across the world to offer their final prayers. It says so much about his teachings that in the aftermath of his passing, the depth of his spirituality blossomed, and his divinity was intensified. It is a legacy that lives and breathes and flourishes, as if he was present in form. And in many ways, to his devotees, he is. The memories are so steeped in genuine fondness and awe that it is as if he never left the surly bonds of earth.

Revisiting his many casual conversations over the years with Pramukh Swami and his prophetic words spoken in 1997, Swami Brahmaviharidas recalls, 'I remember that moment so vividly. I once asked whether it was wise to make a temple in the UAE. We talked about meeting the royal family and directly inquiring about the possibility of building a temple. And I raised an honest doubt about its permanence or long-term existence.'

Pramukh Swami said with an assuring smile, 'Nothing is permanent on earth. Not even the earth. And no one is permanent, not even you. When the time is right, just do it. God will take care of things. When God wills, things happen. Have faith, and trust the leaders of the nation.'

When it was time to write the official letter for a temple, Swami Brahmaviharidas sought guidance from Pramukh Swami. 'There is a dilemma. Some local leaders are of the opinion that the word "temple" should not be mentioned in such a letter. Because to date, no temple has been officially approved. Hence a non-religious phrase such as a "community centre", "meditation centre", "cultural centre" or any such equivalent should be used.'

Pramukh Swami did not hesitate in vetoing the suggestion. His clarity and moral guidance were, 'If you start with a lie, you will end up with a lie. Tell the truth; do not twist it or tweak it. Do not coat, cloak or veneer truth for selfish reasons. Half-truths to get along do not last long. Remember, the bigger the people, the greater they value honesty. So, be pure and simple and straightforward. Say it gently, but say it gracefully. If you want to build a temple, ask for a temple. Search your heart, speak your heart and do the right thing for the right reasons.'

Swami Brahmaviharidas explains, 'Finally, the letter requesting land for a temple was written and sent to HH Sheikh Nahyan and to the Crown Prince of Abu Dhabi, HH Sheikh Mohammed bin Zayed Al Nahyan. A few days later, we received a reply that our request had been approved. Land would be granted in Abu Dhabi. Ironically, the place we once hesitated to visit was now welcoming us. I was not too sure at first, but the sheer grace and generosity of the leadership overwhelmed me. All misgivings gave way to a surge of hope and faith.'

But after that development, there was a lull. All through 2013 and 2014, nothing really moved forward.

A year later, in 2015, Narendra Modi, the Prime Minister of India made a historic trip to the UAE. His closeness to then Crown Prince HH Sheikh Mohammed bin Zayed Al Nahyan allowed for the temple land to be discussed and an official announcement was made on 16 August 2015.* That momentous day deserves elaboration down the line.

The next three years elapsed in turning the announcement into allotment with all the necessary approvals. BAPS swamis and volunteers met with officers and authorities presenting designs and needs. From the Royal Court of the Crown Prince to the Ministry of Foreign Affairs, from the Ministry of Urban Planning to the Department of Community Development, detailed discussions were held and the smallest explanations

---

* 'UAE allocates land for Abu Dhabi's first Hindu temple', *Al Jazeera*, 17 August 2015. Available at: https://www.aljazeera.com/features/2015/8/17/uae-allocates-land-for-abu-dhabis-first-hindu-temple.

were given. Not once, but many times over, because this was the first such temple in Abu Dhabi and in the Middle East. In between, ministers and officers visited the BAPS temple in London and later, the Swaminarayan Akshardham in New Delhi. Both the size of the plot and its location underwent revisions multiple times. Initially, 2.5 acres were gifted in Al Watba along the road from Abu Dhabi to Al Ain. It was later increased to 5 acres and then shifted to the current plot of 13.5 acres with an additional 13.5 for parking. Finally, 27 acres of land in Abu Mureikha on the arterial expressway between Abu Dhabi to Dubai were granted.

Then in the year 2018, Prime Minister Modi returned to the UAE on one of the warmest and friendliest visits by a head of state. For the first time, the Presidential Palace, Qasr Al Watan, was opened to guests and people for his reception. On 10 February, a number of key bilateral memoranda of understanding (MOUs) were signed between the two nations. However, the highlight of the event became the presence of two BAPS swamis—Swami Ishwarcharandas and Swami Brahmaviharidas—who presented the designs of the temple. HH Sheikh Mohammed bin Zayed Al Nahyan, in the presence of Honourable Prime Minister Shri Narendra Modi, chose the traditional stone design for the historic and iconic temple. The meeting was more like a meeting of brothers, a meeting of minds and hearts, as more than a thousand high-profile dignitaries approved and applauded this millennial moment of harmony.

From high above, Pramukh Swami must have nodded his approval for the way his team of swamis moved seamlessly into action.

The high gear was noticeable. When Dr Aman Puri, the Indian ambassador, went to present his credentials in the capital, the first question he was asked referred to the progress of the temple. Earlier, Ambassador Navdeep Suri had a mission. There must be no stone left unturned, literally and figuratively, so that when his tenure was over, he would have the satisfaction of knowing the situation was well under control.

* * *

I visited the site when construction was midway and chatted with the workers who came from all faiths to work as a cohesive team. That day in February 2023, there were over 300 workers on site.

I decided to corral Swami Aksharatitdas and get his take on things. He was the man on the spot for the construction and lived on the site. He is not just likeable, but also quite an authority on a wide range of subjects. Cut from the same cloth as Swami Brahmaviharidas, he exudes the same loping, cheerful demeanour. But once you get to know them, you realize that beneath that affable manner lies a steel core, bordered on each side by a specific trait. On the left is resolve, on the top of the square a sense of commitment, on the right a constancy of conduct and shoring up the base, a conviction for their cause. Over time, you also notice they have a certain stature, and the dynamics change when they enter the room. The younger swami is clearly being mentored and what could be more indicative of trust than placing him in charge of the site? Herein lies another story.

The traditional architect of the temple is Vipul Sompura, and the man in charge of temple construction is Sanjay Parikh, with continual and overall hands-on guidance from Swami Akshaymunidas and Swami Brahmaviharidas. Sanjay has been designing BAPS temples for decades. Swami Aksharatitdas told me when this mandir was being designed, the team under Sanjay travelled around the world to see other buildings, various architectures and other temples, to be adequately inspired and mentally stimulated enough to create a masterpiece.

Aksharatit Swami said, 'And that is why the mandir here is different from any of the temples we have built. That is, 1,600 and counting. If you go anywhere in the world and enter a BAPS temple, you will notice the vast majority of them comprise rectangles, where the main three spires are in one line. But here you are seeing this seven-spired geometric triangular format, where you have a central singular spire that rises from the ground, then two more spires, and then another two, and two spires. Such a multi-spired, geometric and intensely carved stone mandir has not been made anywhere in the last 1,000 or more years. So yes, that one aspect alone makes this temple unique.'

17

No Stone Unturned

'Friends are the sunshine of life. They brighten our days, warm our hearts, and chase away the clouds.'

—Jean Paul

The procurement of stone was a globetrotting journey. Swami Aksharatitdas has a take on it.

'I think, sometimes, to give a sense of a miracle, you must talk about the failures as well. We went to Macedonia and wanted to markup stone and do all of that. Brahmavihari Swami, Sanjay Parikh and I went to quarries, and we looked at stones but saw things we were not so happy with. That was a failed trip and was filed away in our memories. We then went to Greece. We did not want particularly to go to Greece, but one of the volunteers suggested we might as well give it a shot. So we just got a car and drove off. Saw the stone there. It looked good, but then the guy who owns the quarry said, "You probably shouldn't use our stone. It is too soft and won't live up to your structural needs." So, we left a bit dismayed. This search was beginning to turn into an odyssey without end. We had permission to build, but where was the stone? We were in a quandary. Just when we were stressing big time, we received a message from Dr Karzai, President of Afghanistan, through a leading businessman, indicating that he would love to contribute stone to build the temple. But even that act of pure kindness came with its own challenges. The stone would have to go through tough terrains, unsafe roads and unfriendly ports. And because of these thick clouds of uncertainty, we were certain that that was not an option; we could not see it happening. So, that was a non-starter, too. Finally, we came home crestfallen, and then things began to fall into place.'

The BAPS Temple in Abu Dhabi, also known as the 'Mandir', is being constructed using pink sandstone sourced from Rajasthan and white marble from Italy. The intricate carvings and sculptures that adorn the temple were also created in India. Over 4,000 skilled artisans and master craftsmen who specialize in traditional stone-carving techniques, worked night and day to make this miracle in the desert. The stone was shipped to Abu Dhabi and assembled stone by stone.

This pink sandstone, sourced from the town of Bansi Paharpur in the Karauli district, is known for its quality and has been used in the construction of many historic and iconic buildings, including the Red Fort and the Agra Fort in North India.

At the end of March 2023, we decided that a trip to Pindwara in Rajasthan was warranted. Over 2,000 artisans were engaged in the singular art that marks their town and their skill. They are renowned for the exquisite and intricate sculptures they do by hand. If anyone is making a house of worship, first come to Pindwara; it is not an option, but more a mandate.

We planned to land in Ahmedabad and drive over four hours to make it to this pilgrimage of human endeavour.

Two nights before the departure, I balk at the idea, my age manifesting itself rudely. The trek seems arduous and exhausting. Swami Brahmaviharidas registers my self-indulgent reluctance and cancels the trip.

My backing off at the last minute is made to look even more inconsiderate because the chairman of the BAPS temple committee, Ashok Kotecha, is present. He has just lost his mother after a long and courageous battle, and the grief at her departure envelopes him with stoic but still visible despair. A truly good son, he is clearly circling the void and trying to come to grips with the cruel fact. It is like this huge hollow space, and you are shovelling memories to fill it, but it does not fill, and the emptiness stays. Swamis specially visited his home to pray, and Swami Brahmaviharidas sent a text message of love, inner strength and comfort from Africa.

I take the liberty of sharing the contents with you. I strongly feel they encapsulate the priorities of BAPS Swaminarayan spirituality and how they rally round in good times and in times of great distress:

I reach out to you, your wife, your family, your friends and relatives. I know that everyone, including all the swamis, not just respect you but love you deeply and value what you have given to others and society. But amongst all the people that have come into your life, the most important person was the person who brought you into this life . . . your mother. I know how much you loved her and how deeply you respected her. I have seen the way you and your wife have served your mother, never allowing her to lose the dignity she deserved. I also want to reach out and say that all of us were praying, but deep in my heart I always felt that when you and your wife gave her the permission and the assurance that 'Yes mother, Bhagwan Swaminarayan is waiting for you,' and you all were happy to see her happy, she left this earth. Bhagwan Swaminarayan, Yogiji Maharaj, Pramukh Swami Maharaj and Mahant Swami Maharaj have accepted her in their loving arms and given her the place she deserves in the lap of God. She always viewed Guruhari Darshan, and she always felt that Yogiji Maharaj was still alive . . . Pramukh Swami Maharaj is still alive. And that is perhaps the secret for all devotees. You keep your guru alive with the love that you have; and that's the reason all of you should be really smiling that she's reached a place where she is most comfortable in, and she will continue to inspire you. Remember those whom we love, never leave us; they are always there not just as witness but are watching over us. Now is the time not to mourn the passing away of your mother; now is the time to celebrate her life, to live the values she nourished you with and to do her proud as the ideal son. Every step and every breath you take from now onwards is an offering to God and our Guru, and her. You are an ideal son; perhaps you did not take your mother to all the pilgrim places in India or across the world like Shravan, but you were there holding her hand when she breathed her last. The sadhus' prayers were there; I was doing mala continuously. The love of Mahant Swami Maharaj was there. All the family members, Nitinbhai who brought you into satsang, and everybody who loves you, were all there in spirit. I do believe there cannot be a better way to pass on like your mother did. Love is the way forward, devotion to God, dedication to our parents and determination to do the good that all of us want to do is paramount. I wanted to be there with you. I was standing in spirit and mind, and I know you kept feeling it but once I get back the first thing I'll do is to hold you and deeply hug you to tell you that all of us are there for forever.

When you are in that post-loss daze, you do need comfort and sincerity in gestures and words offers you that. Empathy is the need of the cruel hour.

I leave them that day a little heavy in my heart and that afternoon, I have a startlingly clear epiphany.

Was I lazy in cancelling the trip? After all, these are the people whose talent will create for posterity the grandeur and majesty of the temple. Not just the façade but even the sanctum sanctorum. These gifted hands will pour love and care, bringing joy to millions. Their craftsmanship will invoke the gods to acknowledge their art and here I am, mewling over a four-hour car drive replete with snacks and cold drinks.

This happens so often; we tend to overlook the effort of the lower rungs of the ladder, faceless and nameless.

Chinese financial expert Rayner Chua says, 'During Chinese New Year, we celebrate a day called 人日 (Renri) or in literal translation, "Human Day". In Chinese mythology, Renri is the 7th day of the Chinese New Year, when human beings were first created by the goddess Nüwa. It is a day when all of us are reminded of our equal standing as humans in the eyes of our creator.'*

---

* Rayner Chua, 'Deserving Dignity - A tribute to the nameless in our society', LinkedIn. Available at: https://www.linkedin.com/pulse/deserving-dignity-tribute-nameless-our-society-rayner-chua/.

But do we heed that message?

The craftspeople and skilled and unskilled workers, the labourers and the workers of society, are separated by a barrier that might be visible to one side, but is made of granite and is unpassable for the other. These individuals are not part of society; instead, they 'stand apart' from it. And we pay lip service.

Like a leaky valve in a tap, guilt begins to drip into my mind. As if reading it, Swami coincidentally sends me a WhatsApp message. It says, 'Amazing progress. Both the intricately carved traditional stone mandir and the modern monolithic surrounding buildings, are coming up like clockwork. Prayers, passion and perseverance of swamis, volunteers and skilled workers are creating a wonder of art, culture and values – The BAPS Hindu Mandir in Abu Dhabi.'

The drip of guilt gets stronger. I am now berating myself for not going. Is it my arrogance that kept me from making the pilgrimage and seeing the unseen heroes, up front and centre? The ones who do the magic?

And so, I vow to myself that before this book is finished, I will meet them and make it my mission so that no one is unseen, certainly not the princes of Pindwara.

18

To Bee or Not to Bee

*'Take up one idea. Make that one idea your life—think of it,
dream of it, live on that idea.'*
                    —His Holiness Pramukh Swami Maharaj

One afternoon, I go for a swim. A half-dozen honeybees have
fallen in the pool and drowned. A paradox. Bees are so smart,
they make hives and honeycombs and the only food that never
spoils. Then they kill themselves by diving into water. I scoop
them out with a net, and then I notice one bee has just fallen
in and is struggling to save itself, so I rush to it, pull it out and
mere seconds before it would have been forever stilled, I watch
it dry itself in the sun and then fly away.

I feel inordinately good and flushed with a sense of
accomplishment like that glow from doing a good deed.

If I relate this story to Swami Brahmaviharidas, I reckon he
will say, 'Ah, so you felt good, you felt like a god making the
decision to save the bee. You didn't just do it and move on, you

let the ego step in and take a talking part. You see, that is the difference, you do something because that is the right thing to do, not because it gives you an exceptional thrill or because you pat yourself on your back for being a good person.'

That is true humility, when the act is mutually exclusive from the vibration it gives you.

Ergo, you save the bee to save the bee, not because it makes you feel good or makes you feel proud. It's not a badge you win.

Swami has a way of hitting the ball into your court, making you stretch and strengthen your game. He takes the game of life to a new level.

By the same token, he also gives credit with alacrity. As he speaks of the swiftness with which things began to move on the temple front, one name keeps coming up. The Chief of Staff in the Ministry of Foreign Affairs and International Cooperation was a young and very helpful Mohammed Al Khaja. The former Indian Ambassador Navdeep Suri, is clear in acknowledging that Mohammed Khaja was instrumental in keeping the 'temple train' on-track and moving. This young icon of the successful new generation of Emiratis is currently the first-ever Ambassador from the UAE to Israel, a post that underscores his standing and the faith reposed in his capabilities. Born in 1980, Mohammed has four children and holds a degree in political science from Northeastern University in Boston and secured an MBA in Energy Management from Vienna University of Economics and Business.

Before being posted as an envoy, he was a member of the political affairs council and the diplomatic committee, as well as served as the chairman of the budget committee.

A varied career path has taken him to roles in energy management, disarmament and international security, production and procurement management and research and business development for the likes of International Petroleum Investment Company, Borouge Pte. Ltd., Singapore, and Emirates Centre for Strategic Studies and Research.

It is not just the diplomats who hold him in high esteem. The senior swamis in the BAPS organization are happy to say that because of his good offices and his readiness to signpost the right direction, things moved fast and smoothly.

Swami Brahmaviharidas says, 'There were over a hundred different clearances to obtain, from immigration to customs, dispatch of consignments to storage, and without hesitation, it was Mohammed Al Khaja who coordinated our cause.'

'We were thinking of constructing a temple which was not visibly like a traditional temple and would look like any other regular building in Abu Dhabi. Inside would be a prayer hall, like worship places in warehouses. Our attitude was one of accommodation, respecting local sentiments. After all, any place of worship is only as potent as the faith inside it. You might have an elaborate place of worship, but if the people who come are not genuinely faithful, then the transformation and peace that people should feel is never felt.'

When HH Sheikh Abdullah bin Zayed Al Nahyan, Minister of Foreign Affairs and International Cooperation, visited India in June 2018 and held wide-ranging discussions, he visited the Akshardham temple in New Delhi on 26 June and was very impressed.

Upon seeing the sculptures on the elephant plinth and reflecting upon its messages of harmony, patience, strength and wisdom, HH Sheikh Abdullah expressed his happiness at Akshardham's commitment to generate values for generations to come. He appreciated Akshardham's dedication towards water conservation, renewable energy and preservation of art, culture and values.

On entering the mandir, His Highness was fascinated by the intricate carvings and the spirit of the volunteers, stating that their selflessness is 'Incredible . . . In this age and time, volunteerism itself makes Akshardham special'. As HH Sheikh Abdullah's visit came to a close, he took a brief pause on the steps of Akshardham, called Indian Ambassador Navdeep Suri and UAE Ambassador Ahmed Albanna over and said, 'Tell Swami Brahmaviharidas that I took the plans for both of the designs to my brother, who wants the temple in Abu Dhabi to look like a traditional temple.'

The Abu Dhabi paper, *The National*, on 28 June 2018, headlined Sheikh Abdullah's temple visit in India a 'moment in history' and wrote: 'HH Sheikh Abdullah captured the interest of the community who saw his stopover at the temple as an indication of tolerant and peaceful coexistence in the UAE.'

He stayed for two hours and was intrigued enough to seek answers to some of his questions and expressed his opinion that the temple to be built in Abu Dhabi should have the same awe-inspiring architecture and magnificence of Akshardham.

It was perhaps on this day and during this visit that the decision from the rulers of the UAE was reconfirmed. The temple should look like a temple and there was no need to cloak or camouflage. HH Sheikh Abdullah underscored that choice.

* * *

In the BAPS Swaminarayan Sampradaya, they have three types of temples. One is *shikharbaddha mandirs*—traditional stone temples which are designed and constructed as per the ancient shilpashastras, wherein no steel is used, and every stone is assembled like a giant jigsaw puzzle.

The second is *hari mandirs*—regular temples, which are of two types; one with spires made of cement, concrete and steel. The other without spires, which are just normal buildings, with halls and space for assemblies and prayers.

The third is *ghar mandirs* or home altars, where families gather for daily arti and personal prayers.

Swami Brahmaviharidas says, 'Fully cognizant of these parameters, we prepared two plans. The first plan was of a shikharbaddha mandir—a traditional stone temple, which would take four to five years to make, and the other one would be like a hari mandir—a regular building of cement, concrete and glass. That is something we had kept as a viable option. To be very frank, I thought that the easier way to make a mandir without getting into the spotlight would be to make it like a normal building; basic and not standing out from the area's architecture. Before that, I had several discussions with the UAE leadership regarding the importance of emotional infrastructure. A country can have the best of buildings, the best of infrastructure, but until the people who live there are emotionally satisfied, they will not call it their home and will always seek a home elsewhere. To make the UAE their home and feel at home, they need emotional infrastructure. And it is a fact that a big part of emotional infrastructure is spirituality—personal faith, belief and comfort to worship your God.

'It was already felt in these discussions with local leadership that they did value this aspect, but to be able to project it, portray it and put it into action was a challenge. Before PM Modi came here in 2018, we went to Delhi and met him to explain to him that there were some important decisions that needed to be taken.

'It was decided that when the Prime Minister of India visits the UAE, the decision of whether to build a traditional or a regular temple would be taken collectively, in the presence of the Crown Prince, after showing both of them both concepts.

'I thought that this was an appropriate stance. As religious people, life is more about responsibility than rights. Responsibility is what we have and rights, as we perceive them, will take care of themselves. In our world, if we keep shouting for rights without any regard for responsibility, we will lose ourselves. When we display real responsibility, our rights will always be respected. This is human nature. For me, this has always been a guiding beacon, and I will never put this torch down in whatever I do. I tell everyone I meet from any walk of life: be responsible.'

19

Twelve Glorious Minutes

'I ain't never seen the likes since I's been born—how the people keep a-comin' and the train's done gone.'

—Anonymous Stationmaster

There is a spiritual lesson embodied in these words of wisdom of an old stationmaster from an unnamed southern state of America. Our time on earth is short. It won't be long till we must board a train, as it were, bound for the Kingdom of God and eternal life.

God even now, is viewing us on the spiritual track headed for his kingdom. There is not much time left to prepare for departure. Are we going to be on time to board that train, or be among those left behind?

Once it departs, the latecomers who arrive, wring their hands in despair because the train has gone while they have yet to come to terms with their spiritual selves, blinded by the material, fuelled by greed, chasing after false suns.

To catch the train of life, one has to let go of many things and master many more. Vision, effort, awareness, courage, commitment, perseverance, sacrifice, selflessness, compassion, love, integrity, inner values and goodness are all important. But above all is the grace of God.

For any meaningful moment to occur, all of the above are important. However, for a millennial moment that is timeless, multidimensional moments have to align to make magic happen. And this is exactly what happened on 10 February 2018. The stars were aligned.

Says Swami Brahmaviharidas, 'Then came the day we had to catch our own train, albeit a short but vital journey for our expedition. It was a normal day that dawned. But there was nothing normal about it. This is the moment Pramukh Swami had envisioned, and we, as his emissaries, had to march forth and be counted.'

The senior swamis were nervous. The invitation was clear. They had been invited to the palace. Present there would be the Crown Prince of Abu Dhabi and soon to be President of the UAE, HH Sheikh Mohammed bin Zayed Al Nahyan, and he would be hosting Indian Prime Minister Narendra Modi and his official delegation.

Swami Brahmaviharidas recalls every moment with immense clarity, 'We were given instructions on the code of conduct in advance. They told us a certain distance had to be maintained, no questions were to be asked, nor were we permitted to engage in private conversation. There was an official protocol, and it had to be followed to the T. Pujya Ishwarcharan Swami and myself were a little tense in the car, and there was not much conversation because we all knew that this was a major meet regarding the progress of the temple project.'

There were over 1,000 high-profile dignitaries congregated there. The swamis joined the crowd and witnessed the signing of several Indo-UAE bilateral treaties, each concluded to much enthusiastic applause.

Swami Brahmaviharidas says, 'I was uncertain and apprehensive of what would happen. Then the protocol officers instructed us how to walk in and to stand some 50 feet away from the heads of state. That is where the signing tables were, and no one was allowed to move closer.

'I said to the protocol officers that we have to show the Crown Prince the book of concepts. They politely refused saying, "You don't show him anything, you simply don't go close. Hence, pass the book to us, and we will present it to him. This is how it is done."

'I said, "What if the Crown Prince calls us?" They said, "That does not happen," and I said "What if he does?," and I got that sort of "you have to be kidding" look, like that's not gonna happen.'

At this point Prime Minister Modi saw the two swamis, which, truth be told, was not difficult, because of how they stood out in their saffron robes. The PM folded his hands, raised them and from across the hall, greeted them with an audible 'Jai Swaminarayan!'

The protocol officers were puzzled as both the Crown Prince and the prime minister welcomed the swamis with open arms. The swamis and the directors of the BAPS Hindu Mandir covered the distance swiftly and were now meeting the two leaders.

It was an incredible moment, one that has been photographed and framed for posterity to preserve.

The white book of concept held not just by Swami Brahmaviharidas but also by the Crown Prince, who showed interest in every page while the PM talked to Swami Ishwarcharandas. The Crown Prince avidly listened to Swami Brahmaviharidas explain the two concepts of which he approved the traditional temple. That is when the PM told Swami Brahmaviharidas that the Crown Prince and he are like brothers, to which the Crown Prince added, while pulling Swami Brahmaviharidas closer, that they are all brothers. What a royal way of approving the temple with a legacy of love and harmony!

From no go to a courtesy meet, to a full-fledged interaction in one fell swoop.

From the video footage, it is clear that the meeting was natural, spontaneous and fulfilling. No one interrupted them in front of that high-profile congregation which continued to applaud. It did not last a couple of minutes but went on for for twelve glorious minutes.

As they left, both swamis realized that this was a watershed moment in the saga that had begun on the sands of Sharjah in 1997. This temple would be built.

The good mood drove back with them in the car. And as the sun went down on the day, there was so much light in the Jaffiliya residence where Swamiji was staying, as the details of the meeting were shared with the others. It was as if Pramukh Swami had done some talking with the sun and told it to stay up in the sky and shine on.

20

Engineer Par Excellence

'A doctor can bury his mistakes, but an architect can only advise his clients to plant vines and trees.'

—*Frank Lloyd Wright*

It is a sun-kissed day in April, and the weather in Dubai is turning. Mercury has hopped from a glorious 21°C to 28°C, and summer is nigh.

Work at the site of the temple is a little slower because of the time limits in the holy month of Ramadan. Even so, progress is like you see a child doing a 1,000-piece jigsaw puzzle; the pieces are falling into place—the façade, the pillars, the columns, the arches, the filigree and the eternally frozen sacred animals sculpted with chisels tipped with love. All of it as finely tuned as a symphony orchestra readying for the curtain to rise in February 2024.

One of the conductors is Sanjay Parikh, a genius in his own right, the composer of the construction symphony. We are engaged in a voyage of discovery. His story is riveting.

He says, 'When I finished my master's degree from IIT Kanpur in 1989, I came to Ahmedabad to see Pramukh Swami Maharaj like I often did. I met him and explained that I had finished my education. Before that, in 1987, when I was studying in Kanpur, Pramukh Swami Maharaj had visited Uttarakhand to do the Char Dham yatra. He came to Delhi at that time, where he stayed for a week, accompanied by about 350 swamis en route to Kolkata. For some reason, he allowed me to stay with him. I spent some good time with him, and I must say, he treated me like his own son.'

So why this affection for Sanjay?

'I don't know exactly, but he asked me about my education and how I was managing my dietary restrictions, not eating any onion and garlic. I told him that in our hostel, they regularly made boiled *sabji* and dal for those who are sick, and that is what I would eat with curd and rice. He was happy that I was following my *niyams*.

'So, right after I finished my education, I thought it would be best to meet with Swamishri before I decide what I want to do next. He was happy and said, "We are constructing an Akshardham temple in Gandhinagar. Why don't you go there and help Swami Akshaymunidas who is looking after the project?"

Sanjay jumped at the opportunity.

'This was in 1989. I happily went and joined the Akshardham team. Then I received the seva of overseeing various engineering aspects. I have specialized in geotechnical engineering, which is a part of civil engineering. So, it deals with soil and foundations.'

Who more qualified to get things started? Pramukh Swami's legendary foresight manifested itself again.

'When I was doing the seva in Gandhinagar Akshardham, Pramukh Swami Maharaj would often come. That is where I would get a chance to meet him, to explain certain technicalities. The Gandhinagar Akshardham project was completed in 1992. At that time, talk of the London temple had begun and I was co-opted. I loved that project very much because when the architects and the engineers we had selected from the UK came to India to study how temples were made, I became the bridge between their modern techniques and our ancient knowledge. They could not grasp how structures of this size could be made without any steel or metal.'

Sanjay's expertise also lies in finding the right stone. This is not as easy as it might sound.

'I visited quite a few places to find the right stone for Gandhinagar. For the London mandir, we selected stones from Bulgaria and Italy. I got a chance to visit these countries and explore the best options. And now Abu Dhabi is taking it to a new level.

'There are quite a few things which make the BAPS Hindu Mandir in Abu Dhabi special. The first thing is that all of these BAPS mandirs in which I was involved had five *shikhars* and five sanctums. When we started to design this mandir, the concept was very clear that we are designing a Hindu mandir that will enshrine the major deities of India. Hence, we wanted to include art from different regions of India. For this, we studied the temples of Jagannathji, Konark, Ranakpur, Delwara and lots of other places of worship throughout India. We wanted to make sure that the BAPS Hindu Mandir in Abu Dhabi represents the temple art and architecture of entire India. Moreover, episodes from the *Ramayana, Mahabharata, Bhagavatam, Shiva Purana, Swaminarayan Charitram* and the lives of Tirupati and Ayyappan, too, have been carved. It also includes value tales from ancient civilizations of the world. If you see the different features of this mandir, they represent not just the different regions of India but different cultures of the world. And that makes it more than unique.'

And Sanjay has a final take that is an impressive dimension in itself.

'Do you remember when there was an earthquake on the Iran–Iraq border? At that time, all the Gulf Cooperation Council (GCC) countries made strong policies about how their buildings should be constructed. We had to make sure that we complied with their standards, and our most important task was to make our structure earthquake-resistant without the use of any steel. So, we had to perform some engineering feats to meet the required codes.

'Ultimately, it was proved that our mandir could withstand an earthquake, even of the magnitude of the Bhuj earthquake.

'How do we know this? We have performed special tests on the stones, constructed mathematical models, digitally simulated seismic forces, and for the first time in history, we have installed 300 sensors to provide live data. When Mahant Swami Maharaj came to know of this, especially the fact that now we are able to prove the principles of ancient engineering through modern technology, he asked me to do further research in this field. I happily took that challenge and now I am doing a PhD on the correlation between modern engineering and ancient structures.'

There goes a very special man . . . Sanjaybhai Parikh, an engineer par excellence.

21

Architect with That Exquisite Touch

'Let the beauty of what you love be what you do.'

—*Rumi*

Like most things with BAPS, simplicity is the key to decision-making. If you cannot find a good reason to reject, then just accept. That's exactly how it went with the Dubai branch of the company RSP, whose slogan is an intriguing 'Design Re-imagined'. Singapore-based, it has, in the past sixty years, established its credentials in the field of architectural design and execution.

Prabhanjan Kambadur, a director at RSP, shares how it all went down. His senior, the MD of the Middle East offices, Michael Magill, had never been involved in designing a house of worship. Malls, stadiums, condos, yes, but a temple, not once. It was a normal day at work when a client engineered a meeting with Swami Brahmaviharidas and Swami Aksharatitdas, and at that time, I think, they were going to finalize the design. At that time, Jasbir Singh Sahni was leading the project.

Prabhanjan says, 'This crucial meeting was held at the home of Yogesh Mehta, owner of Petrochem, who is also the vice chairman of the BAPS Hindu Mandir committee. We showed them our portfolio, and they said, "Okay, why don't you make something?," and that is how we began work on the initial design. Michael then did the concept of the spiritual oasis in the desert; I think they liked it.

'One thing that stood out was that this is a legacy project. It is going to leave a legacy, not just in Abu Dhabi, not just in the UAE, but also probably in the whole world, because it is the first, like you say, shikharbaddha temple in this part of the world. Apart from that, it is a place that will be visited by a lot of people. At RSP, we have a lot of projects where we have a lot of visitors. We have dealt with that aspect, but not in the context of a temple. For us it was very interesting; as architects, we always like to feel challenged. When this proposal came through, we were all excited.

'It was all so new in the client–architect equation. Typically, we deal with commercial clients, and the clients usually say, "I want to build this, and I want to get this much in returns, can you get it done in this size and these constraints and this is the budget." Here, the brief was singular. What is it you can do that can make this a legacy project? We were not dealing with managers, we were dealing with devotees; we were dealing with swamis.

'Things happen for a reason. There is a cause and effect. Just at that time, our global MD, Mr Lai, came on a visit to Dubai by sheer chance. It was unscheduled. We introduced him to the BAPS team, and they hit it off splendidly. He was deeply touched by their simplicity and selflessness. When we came out of the meeting, the MD said, "Guys let's just do it, don't worry about the fees."

'And we didn't.

'Now, it was time to travel to India. I had been to Ahmedabad, but not other places in Gujarat. Our journey started off at the Swaminarayan Akshardham, Delhi. Then we went to the Swaminarayan Akshardham in Gandhinagar. From there, we went to see several temples. Some were under construction, some already finished. We stayed in the ashram, we ate the food, and I think by the fourth day, Michael was saying, "Okay, why do you guys eat so many chickpeas?"

'But he enjoyed it as well. Michael and I have worked together for the past fifteen years on so many projects. But every time, it was just go stay at a hotel, go to the office, finish the meeting and get out. This was more like a complete immersion. What struck us most forcefully was that everyone involved from the BAPS side is not an employee and getting paid for it—they are dedicated volunteers. Now when I see what we imagined in blueprints and sketches and compu-graphics becoming a reality, it is an emotional rollercoaster. You feel God gave you a gift, and you must protect it. I don't think for the rest of my career I will do anything else that will come even close to this, unless of course, BAPS asks us to help with another temple . . . and I will jump at it.

'Let me take you to that magical day in Sarangpur. It is as deeply chiselled in my mind as the marble sculptures done by the artisans in Pindwara. Swami Brahmaviharidas sat us down outside on the steps of the Shastriji Maharaj Smruti Mandir in Sarangpur. He asked us to contemplate, "What is the inspiration? What is the story?"

'We had the spiritual oasis, but what else comprised the story; what was the spiritual story in this? Swamiji quietly said, "We must tell a story." Then, he intuitively took Michael's sketch book and sketched three rivers with the mandir in the middle. Elaborating the idea, he explained the importance of the three holy rivers, Ganga, Yamuna and Saraswati. And where they meet becomes the oasis from where the temple should emerge. "It will be an oasis for everyone, a place to find peace and tranquility of body, mind and soul."

'You come here and even if you do not seek it, you discover the history of past civilizations, the folklore of vastly different human entities, the direct connection with your God, a communication that can be silent or unmuted. You find sanctuary in the workmanship and the music, you feel thrilled to be there; the temple must captivate, not capture; it must elevate not deviate; it must let you leave a better person. Every part of this temple has its story to tell, every stone sends out a message of love and tolerance. It should become a spiritual oasis for global harmony.'

And so the journey of harmony continues not just in architecture but in the lives it has touched. An unending saga of devotion and divinity, with many station stops on the way to replenish one's energies, but no ultimate stop. For there can be no end to the eternal.

Sometimes, you leave the best for the last. It is a human compulsion.

22

The Unending Flow of Sheer Genius

'Every block of stone has a statue inside it, and it is the task of the sculptor to discover it. I saw the angel in the marble and carved until I set him free.'

—*Michelangelo*

Indian tourists love going to Mount Abu. This tiny hill station in the Aravalli range is just under two hours' drive from Udaipur airport, so it is well-connected. Summer homes are now very popular, and the holiday destination is an ideal place to unwind. You can sail on the Nakki Lake or seek spiritual serenity by paying homage at the centuries-old Delwara Temples, ornately carved from white marble and of great historical importance.

Just about an hour's downhill drive, there lies the small town of Pindwara. Two aspects to this dusty little township make it stand out as a symbol of what man can do. It is home to master craftsmen who, generation after generation, have dedicated their lives to marble carving and the creation of exquisite divinities for adorning temples and other shrines. Whether it is the pantheon of Hindu gods, revered animals or the telling of a story through a series of sculptures, these men are blessed with great artistic talent. That several thousand of them live in the same area, is an incredible grace and must come from way up on high. What are the odds of 10,000 Michelangelos or 500 Shakespeares or 100 Valmikis living as neighbours and sharing the shade of the same trees? Can you have 100 Tagores writing poetry and prose of grand thought in a township in Kolkata?

Yet, the tradition survives and is handed down from grandfather to father to son. Whole families for generations have linked their livelihood to the making of these exquisite sculptures. Referring to them as experts in marble carving does not come anywhere near defining the reality of their precision and the beauty they can capture with their hands. Nothing has changed over the centuries. Not the eagle eye, not the steady hand, not the simple chisel, just the blessing of being able to bring alive from within cold marble, the image of God.

These skilled artisans were the backbone of an extraordinary project: the construction of a magnificent Hindu temple in Abu Dhabi. It is these craftsmen who leave you spellbound as they transform blocks of pristine marble into breathtaking architectural masterpieces.

Their love affair with the stone dates back to the mid-seventeenth century. The region falls in the Sirohi kingdom and was ruled in the fourteenth century by Rao Devraj, who belonged to the Chouhan community of the Rajputana clan. At that time, Pindwara was known as Pindaravak.

There is also a very ancient history of the Jain community existing in Pindwara, who have been local residents and Bhamashahs (Generals) of Pindwara. In historical times, there is evidence of Jain gurus residing here and the mythological name of Pindwara, Pindaravak, is also mentioned in ancient Jain texts.

It could well be this community that sparked the beginning of the rich legacy we see today. The quarries surrounding Pindwara and its 30,000 inhabitants are of high-grade marble. Even the Ram Mandir in Ayodhya is being given benediction from this little village, as is the BAPS Hindu Mandir in Abu Dhabi.

Using their traditional hand tools, which include chisels and hammers, they carefully carve intricate motifs, delicate filigree work and grand sculptures. Every time the chisel strikes the marble, little chips fly and clouds of marble dust cover the craftsmen's arms and faces, yet they soldier on with dedication, love in their hearts and a reverence that touches the heart of the spectator. Truly, they believe this gift has come from above, and it is their bounden duty to drench their work with pure, unalloyed adoration. Like a magical trick, the figure emerges, almost ethereal in its perfection. Was it really hiding in that block of marble, freed from its stony prison by the genius of the chisel and the rasp?

In many ways, they are preserving Indian history and Hindu spirituality. You cannot but be moved by their commitment and their unwavering desire to create a corridor between the devotee and the divine.

With technology and city lights luring away the young, it is a moot question whether the next 'artificial intelligence' generation will continue this tradition. And if they do, will the instruments change and will robots do the sharp but soulless cutting? The magical element here is the imperfection; that human factor where, on closer scrutiny, every one of the thousand similar figures is infinitesimally and charmingly different and yet, the same.

It is already happening, in that progress cannot be stopped. But even as the tools change, the devotion stays constant. The Abu Dhabi temple is special because it enables these craftsmen to become ambassadors of their country. This profound responsibility is well understood. Not only are they continuing the traditions of their forefathers, but they are showcasing their genius—for genius it is—to the world. This temple will be a testament to their greater glory and bring every visitor closer to the goal of cultural unity.

So with all this history in mind, we get into a conversation with a group of the artisans, even as they are engrossed in their work.

Q. For how many generations has your family been engaging in this work?
A. This work has been passed down for generations. We are not sure exactly when it started, but I have acquired this knowledge from my father, who learned from his father and he from his father. This, I know because they speak about it.

Q. All of you are so skilled. Have you trained as children or does this capability come to you naturally?
A. Like we had said, we learned all of this from our fathers and our brothers, who had done and continue to do this. We start at a good age, when we are young; however, we had always seen our fathers do this work, so it was easier when we started to pick it up. Much is learned by just watching and listening to them share their experiences.

Just like our parents were with us, we don't force our children to continue in this same line. If they feel they are naturally inclined to engage in this career, then we are happy, and if they feel as if they would like to pursue some other line, we are equally happy. As God has willed.

Q. Do you get any special satisfaction or comfort from making these beautiful sculptures?

They give us an 'are you kidding', quizzical look.

A. There is comfort that we are doing this work for God. We actually do not even think of this as work; we think of this as seva. If you ask any of us here on-site, even in casual talk, no one refers to this as work. We all think of it as seva to God . . . which is service to the Lord.

Q. You believe this skill is a gift from God? Does it make you feel blessed?

Their response is a chorus of common purpose.

A. We definitely feel it is all a blessing from God and that God has given us the freedom and space to develop ourselves. Whenever we are stuck—and it happens—we know that God is with us. So, all in all, this is a blessing from God, but without a doubt, it still requires hard work and perseverance to hone this craft and apply it to mandirs of this level.'

To think of them as simple people, and then to walk into the mandir and see its majesty and magnificence—it takes your breath away. It is difficult to reconcile the stunning brilliance on the walls and the façade as the endeavour of an unseen and often unacknowledged group of people who take a chisel and make miracles every single day.

The temple will open its doors to the world on schedule. You can set your watch to that promise. The monks of this mission take time and punctuality very seriously. Every moment is precious.

And when the mandir opens, it will not only be a house of worship, but a home for learning. That is the premise which is at the core of this groundbreaking venture. There will be grand thought, even grander debate and discourse, people will come to share and to give and to take away an experience in sheer unalloyed goodness in this oasis of serenity and serendipity.

The first such move in the hands across the ocean of motivation was seen in May 2023, when the ambassadors (and their families) of thirty nations residing in the UAE were hosted by the BAPS family and given a tour of the temple as it was being built.

Educationalist Umesh Raja, who covered the visit, said succinctly: 'The dedicated directors and volunteers overseeing the mandir's construction warmly welcomed more than eighty-five esteemed guests. The dignitaries were adorned with garlands and welcomed with the traditional tying of a sacred thread.

'The ambassadors were given a comprehensive overview of the mandir's historical significance, construction process and expected impact, conveyed through captivating video presentations and personal experiences.

'Swami Brahmaviharidas warmly welcomed the ambassadors and their families, "Celebrating the past, calibrating the present and creating the future, BAPS Hindu Mandir amalgamates ancient art and architecture, modern science and technology, universal values and spirituality. Your presence here sends a hopeful message of harmony and is a testament to the belief that dialogue, exchange and engagement can bring us all closer together and make this world a happier place.'"

Perhaps a hundred years from today, when time has given the stones a new sheen and the staying power has maintained the temple's pristine condition, there will emanate from its walls that sense of togetherness and unity, and indeed, tolerance, that in the third decade of the twenty-first century were commodities in short supply.

And as for its presence and its role—the world will be a better place.

23

In the Aftermath

'Great things are done by a series of small things brought together.'

—*Vincent Van Gogh*

They are assorted like chocolates in a gift box. Right through the months of writing this book, I never ceased to be amazed by the joyous texture of the volunteers' commitment. And the consummate ease with which they gave up their corporate and professional lifestyles, with all the status symbols cast aside, and no regret. Educationalists, corporate honchos, fast-tracked careerists, college grads dropping Ivy League positions, engineers, scientists, photographers, artists—you can find them all among the volunteers, putting their salaries on hold for months; a year or indefinitely. Nothing has amazed a layman like me more than this untrammelled devotion. I feel a mix of emotions. When I started this book, I was inclined to needle them and push their buttons.

The young lot—don't you want a beer, a girlfriend, watch movies, go to a cricket match, have fun? You are twenty years old.

The middle-aged guys who walked away from all the wealth accumulated over their careers—you could be MDs, put a footstep in the private sector's corridors of power. Why have you taken long-term sabbaticals to sit here day after day and serve this godly organization?

The older lot—retired and semi-retired, almost like me, tottering into antiquity and yet full of intent and resolve.

Colleagues helping me—with the writing bookended by Hari Patel, a super-genius youngster and someone whom you can't help but like. The young photographer, Sagar Rathod, dedicated to that camera and inexhaustible in his approach to the day's work. On the other side, Umesh Raja, a man of many hues with the most dramatic top-shelf career as a teacher and headmaster, so reminiscent of the legendary film, *To Sir, with Love*. His peers love the man, and it is easy to see why. What they write about him would make a reader blush with pride.

My admiration is grudging, like I am in a mental tug of war. If I admire too much but cannot follow, is there a failing in me? Do they see something I cannot see? I do not mock, because I never mock or jeer anyone, but off and on, they make me feel inadequate, and so, I won't let the rope go this easy. Make your own assessment. Walk with me as I talk to some of these individuals who have been pillars in the building of the extraordinary temple.

Two of them left the mortal coils far too soon. Rohit Patel was much loved and with his passing, the BAPS congregation lost a great ally. His sons and grandchildren keep the flag aloft.

The other major loss was that of Jasbir Singh Sahni in 2021. As the project director, he worked 24/7 to make the dream come true. He often quoted his guru, saying that the temple will last a thousand years and that is how the title of my own effort was decided: a thousand years; a millennial moment.

Few people know that this is the first time in history a traditional Hindu temple has been fully digitally modelled and put through such extreme seismic simulations. Also, more than 300 sensors have been embedded at different levels to provide live data of changes in temperature, pressure, movement, and stress upon the temple structure.

Let's start walking then and meet these rainmakers, wave makers, news makers—call them what you will; some are devotees, some are volunteers, some are well-wishers, and some are strangers. But they all stood up for the cause of harmony and thus have been counted.

Once Upon a Helipad

Unlike fixed-wing aircrafts that see a ribbon of concrete runway stretching before them, helicopters are not afforded that luxury. Often, the pilot must fly by what is called the seat of his pants and second-guess his destination. Unmarked fields, farm driveways and entrances, livestock crossing areas and farm vehicles, absence of roads can contribute to confusion. Since terrain is often similar, landing on an H-pad not properly marked, can have the chopper land on another spot in the vicinity.

So, why this lesson in aviation? What on earth has it got to do with the festival of harmony and the visitation by thousands to the Wall of Harmony that welcomes you to the mandir?

The 47-metre-long 3D-printed wall is one of the largest in the region and is guaranteed to stand the test of time.

Now, let us explore the connection between this wall, the helicopter and the sunny afternoon of 2 February 2020. After delivering an inspiring keynote address at the headquarters of Hindustan Zinc in Udaipur, the next afternoon, Swami Brahmaviharidas was to be flown by the company's helicopter to Ahmedabad, for the inauguration of Savvy Sports Centre in the presence of the Chief Minister of Gujarat. Timing was critical. As the path of the chopper flew over the area where the stones for the Abu Dhabi Mandir were being carved, Swami requested if the helicopter could be landed in or near the remote village of Sagvada for two hours, so he could see the work and meet the craftsmen. It was all on the fly. Instant and spontaneous. The pilot juggled a flurry of messages and communicated with the local authorities. Onboard were Swami Brahmaviharidas, Swami Atmavatsaldas and Swami Aksharpremdas, leaving Udaipur and en route to the village of Sagvada.

Since the location was remote and not mapped, the pilot fortuitously brought the chopper down in another place quite far away from the requested destination. An error of navigation for some, a grand occasion by accident for others. So it would pan out. It landed in the premises of the Dargah of Fakhruddin Al Shaheed (R.A.), a holy mosque of Bohri Muslims in Galiakot, Rajasthan. The pilgrims and the faithful nearby, hearing the clatter of the chopper, gathered to see what was happening. Not often that unscheduled choppers fetch up in this rural area, so there is, understandably, a frisson of excitement. In this case, there is another special reason.

'God's grace or mistake, our pilot got the different helipads there mixed up,' says Swami.

'This was a very famous village in the area with a very large *dargah*. I see so many Muslim villagers standing there, ready with garlands in their hands. I am not sure what I should do. Should I walk out, stay in the cabin or take off again? There is a fairytale-like atmosphere on the scene . . . as if we were in some unknown land. I step out to this incredible welcome. They garland us, and I put the chadar on the dargah and pray. Our pilot had actually made a mistake . . . or had the hand of God steered us to this spot?'

Fast forward to Expo 2020 in Abu Dhabi. Swami Brahmaviharidas is looking for somebody who could make a 3D-printed model of the BAPS Hindu Mandir, because they were asked to create an exhibit of the mandir for the expo. He walks into Muffadal Ali's office, a small private enterprise with a reputation for making the finest 3D models. Again, coincidence or destiny's orders?

What happened after is best described by Muffadal himself: 'My brother-in-law had related to me the story of a swami landing in my village in a chopper and paying his respects at the dargah. This rendition had been circulated around our community. Just two days earlier, my brother-in-law had been talking to me about this visit and then when Swami came into my office, he asked me where I was from and when I said it was a village close to Galiakot where there is a large dargah, Swami said, "Oh really, once our helicopter landed near that place!"

'And I said, "Wow! I was just talking to my brother-in-law about you yesterday, so you are *that* Swami?!"' And there you are, destiny played her role to the hilt.

With joy, Muffadal Ali printed the mandir model. Yet, when approached for payment, he graciously declined. What were the chances these two would meet like this? And then go on establish a strong bond—thanks to a wrong helicopter landing that was so right.

* * *

It is May 2023. Ambassadors from over thirty nations decide to visit the site of the BAPS Hindu Mandir. It is decided that each ambassador will be gifted a miniature model of the mandir. They approach Muffadal Ali again, who agrees to 3D print fifty models for them. The mandir again asks Muffadal about his payment, yet once again, he declines; this time for a more profound reason. He reveals that it was his mother who had said, 'They are men of God doing seva to society. Serve them selflessly.'

Now the mandir is nearing completion. Swami Brahmaviharidas had an idea of creating a 'wall of harmony' to greet the visitors as they entered the mandir. Unexpectedly, Swami gets a call from an unknown person; his name was Badari.

Swami says, 'That day, one of the people present there when the chopper landed—also a person close to their Guru Sayedna—was Badari. He had never met me, had never come to the mandir, but his brother had once come to the site.'

Badari says, 'Swamiji, while we were in Cairo with our guru, receiving the highest civilian award, we were just talking about you; that you must have angels around you, angels protecting you for the work you are doing. A mandir in the Middle East is unimaginable. You and your achievements are simply amazing.'

On that phone call, Badari expresses his desire to contribute to the mandir. He finds out about Swami's noble idea of having a 'wall of harmony', as explained in his own words: 'Normally, walls divide, but walls also allow you to climb them, rise and see beyond. That is what this wall represents; that we welcome the world with harmony.' That wall is 150 feet long and 15 feet high. Badari and Muffadal Ali took it upon themselves to 3D print the wall in seva as charity. It is one of the largest 3D-printed walls in the UAE.

Imagine as you walk into the mandir, the first welcome note has been made possible by the efforts of the Dawoodi Bohra Muslim community. Talk about harmony . . .

Rohitbhai the Rock

Rohitbhai Patel lost a courageous sixty-day battle with COVID-19 in 2021. He was arguably the strongest and most ardent disciple of the Swaminarayan faith in Dubai, and the man who eased the way for its members to establish their presence in the city and find comfortable living quarters here, where they could reside and address congregations. The complex in Jaffiliya was allotted for this purpose and history will confirm that it will always be seen as the Dubai home for the faith. That significance will make it a place of pilgrimage for every devotee, for it is from here that Pramukh Swami set the ball in motion after praying for a temple.

From the end of the century, this edifice was literally the forerunner of the temple that is being constructed. Evening arti, satsangs, sermons—all of these have been intrinsic to this structure.

So, it is natural that we impose on the Patel family, whose gift it was. Rohitbhai's twin sons Chirag and Chirayu have taken over the mantle from their father and wherever he is watching them from, he must be proud of their priorities. The

children of both sons play tennis at a level that will see them
compete someday soon at Wimbledon and Roland Garros—
they are that good. The same discipline, purposefulness and
drive marks their lives and their game as it does those who
elect to join BAPS. Chirayu welcomes us into his beautiful
home with disarming warmth. The interview dissolves into
genial conversation. Chirayu is extremely forthcoming. The
family's closeness to the Swaminarayan cadres goes back three
generations and maybe even more. He is fully aware of his
grandfather being a devotee in the 1950s, and they grew up in
a home where prayer and discourse and godliness were integral
to their day. Their mother was also a dedicated Swaminarayan
follower. Shastriji Maharaj gave Rohitbhai's grandfather
Dahyabhai Patel much attention and affection. And Pramukh
Swami continued to give that love to Purushottambhai Patel,
Rohitbhai's father, and his two sons, Manubhai and Rohitbhai.
It was natural to witness monks in the house and the gravitation
to their orbit was a given.

Rohitbhai must have been an exceptional man, and he
certainly gave his children the right breeding. They, in turn,
hope they are doing the same with their children, providing
them with a durable and deeply ingrained value system.

'We don't push them,' says Chirayu. 'We guide them, but
we let them choose their own pace of commitment. They are
good kids, they will do the right thing.'

Rohitbhai's persona even pierced Swami Brahmaviharidas's
armour, in that whenever he speaks of Rohitbhai, it is with
so much love and esteem that his voice breaks with emotion.
For a monk who is good at controlling his feelings, this is one
name he cannot help but drench in tenderness, and his voice
drops by an octave. He has lost a good friend and comrade, and

comfort can be found only in memories and the happy fact that the legacy continues; and that the children, like good fruit, have fallen close to the tree.

Right through the turn of the century, Rohitbhai and his family played host to the stream of monks visiting Dubai and it became an accepted fact that the Patel family would ensure their comfort. From 1994 until now and onwards, this service has been a family forte.

Chirayu shares his view on the temple and its progress, having been integral to it from day one: 'I always felt that what was missing here was a place where Indian culture could be celebrated. The farsightedness that the leaders here have shown in getting involved and encouraging this addition is worthy of gratitude, and every one of us must appreciate this. I give credit to Swami Brahmaviharidas for being the catalyst in projecting not just the BAPS doctrine, but the cogent arguments he put forward over the years that produced so much credibility. He is truly the finest ambassador for order and the leaders here accord him so much courtesy. When they meet, it is informal; they are like friends and the conversation has the thrust and riposte of wit and lightness, and it is a privilege to be witness to these meetings. Eminent leaders such as HH Sheikh Mohammed bin Zayed, HH Sheikh Abdullah, HH Sheikh Nahyan have made such an impact with their support and guidance. Think of it, HH Sheikh Abdullah said, "Make a temple but make sure it looks like a temple."'

It is, for many of the stalwarts, a dream come true.

'We are looking forward to the opening in February. I believe the temple campus will attract not just followers, but even tourists. A place of pilgrimage, a place for academic learning, a must on every itinerary.'

With an expected inflow of 7,000–10,000 visitors a day, the prediction of numbers could only be flawed for being on the lower side.

Come 14 February 2024, the Patel brothers and their families will honour Rohitbhai, their father, and his dedication by being up there, front and centre.

And suffice it to say, Rohitbhai will be watching.

More Than an Asset to the Team

With people like him and Ashok Kotecha at the helm of affairs, Swami Brahmaviharidas has little to worry about.

Every now and again, you come across that rare individual who hides his light under a bushel and is easily underestimated. He is neither slick nor stylish and is most happy ensconced in the back rows, away from the glare of publicity. Yet, by sheer virtue of his wit and wisdom, he tends to grow on you until one special moment, when you realize his worth as a person who is not just an asset to a team but a man who delivers, and then some.

Very much like the glass containers he manufactures on a mass scale, Ashok Kotecha is crystal clear in his transparency, durable yet with a certain delicacy, strong yet flexible to fit any shape and size that is required. The sort of person that you will not call indispensable (because he would be the first to deny this label) but difficult to ever replace once you have co-opted him into your midst. Like the words of the song, 'You just call out my name / I'll come runnin' / You've got a friend', his willingness to be of help is visible, be it friends or strangers knocking on his door.

Life was not easy for Ashok. A refugee from Uganda following the Idi Amin act of hostility against expats, he was once a penniless and jobless non-entity in a refugee camp in Naples, Italy. A time when there seemed to be no prospects of any breakthrough and the horizon was dark and bleak. But the Kotecha core was forged in a hard crucible, and he was a fighter even then. He never gave up. Somewhere out there, he knew there was a calling and once released from the camps, he set out to write his own way forward.

A Hindu by birth and hailing from a conservative background where his mother exercised a great deal of influence in creating a value system, Ashok was the quintessential 'good son'. Until the very last day when she left the mortal coil, he cared for her not out of duty but out of love. His dedication to her well-being touched many friends who were witness to the depth of that relationship.

Today, he is the chairman of the BAPS temple committee in the UAE and the man who partners with the senior swamis in generating funding for this milestone house of worship. He goes about his job quietly, with a certain honesty of intent, never forcing the pace or pushing the envelope to the edge. One of his most endearing traits is his ability to empathize and appreciate the other person's limitations. He once said, 'We are all co-passengers on this esoteric journey of life, and it is our duty to be there for one another.'

This ability to walk in other people's shoes and experience where it pinches he would probably credit to his exposure to the Osho movement and his closeness to the Acharya Rajneesh doctrine. He is still an advocate and loyalist as far as those teachings are concerned. And this association was a factor in his first meeting with Pramukh Swami. Ashok had settled in Dubai and was building a life, brick by brick, as a family man and a good neighbour. He had an uncle in

Rajkot who was a great follower of the Swaminarayan faith. Sometime in 1994, he was introduced to Pramukh Swami in London.

Being the upfront person that he is, he confessed he was an Osho disciple and Pramukh Swami smiled and said, 'Oh, we have no issue with that. You are welcome to hold your beliefs.' That is how it all began.

And he hasn't left since. In 1997, he was integral to the now famous trek to the deserts of Sharjah, where Pramukh Swami prayed for peace in the world and for a temple to be built in Abu Dhabi.

'I will never forget that day. It is printed indelibly in my mind. We had driven up in seven cars. The sun was setting, there was a certain surreal tranquility, even though the breeze was quite powerful. We were gathered in a circle and then suddenly, Pramukh Swami decided that such a prayer here would have relevance. And it did . . . twenty-six years later.'

There is another poignant dimension to this period. It had been astrologically predicted that Ashok would pass on in tragic circumstances. So, he was also wrestling with his own demons. Whatever the level of logic or its absence in such pronouncements, the dark cloud of doubt and dread hovers over your head. Ashok elected to share these concerns with Pramukh Swami and seek his counsel.

Pramukh Swami told him to have faith in God and held his hands. It is only later, much later, after the predicted so-called dangerous period had ended, that Ashok realized Pramukh Swami had been by his side right through it, till the last day. In an undefined way, the experience and the nearness of death has given Ashok a *joi de vivre* that is infectious and carefree enough for him to joke about it.

These exposures to the Swaminarayan tradition and its senior monks were soaked in mutual goodwill, but the major turning point for Ashok occurred when he witnessed the role its members played in the aftermath of the Gujarat earthquake. The devastation was shattering and the human agony palpable. These dedicated monks had such an efficient delivery system, whether it was food, clothing, medicine or even words of comfort, they turned night to day being of immense support and asked for nothing in return. Not even gratitude.

Ashok recalls how he and other volunteers steered all the tangible help that people gave through their channels. A ship at the Kandla port owned by the Adanis was offloaded of its cargo and all the relief containers placed onboard and dispatched to the stricken state. The situation in Gujarat was heartbreaking, but the adversity brought Ashok closer to Pramukh Swami and, through these terrible times, to Swami Brahmaviharidas.

Today, the former refugee from the Naples camp is not only a major pillar in the saga of the temple being built in Abu Dhabi, but also one of the most respected and liked individuals on the frontlines. You feel comfortable with him, and his grace and demeanour are disarming. His natural reticence to being celebrated generates a charm of its own. The balance he has created between his functions in the mission and his private and official life is exquisite, even as it underscores a rare stamina. He works a full day at a Saudi Arabian corporation, travels extensively, yet has time to attend to his duties with reference to the temple, and after that, be a family man, getting home in time for them.

No wonder one begins to gravitate towards him and enjoy his company. A one-man band, that is Ashok Kotecha for you, and as Swami Brahmaviharidas might say, 'No man is an island, but Ashok is a continent.'

The Marvel of the Marble Man

It is not Sagoon Patel's first rodeo, having been instrumental in the Neasden project in London and made a massive success of it. He was up front and right there during the making of the temples in Chicago, Toronto, Houston and Atlanta.

Born into a family that was immersed in the Swaminarayan tradition, it was an easy leap for Sagoon to make when he took a three-year sabbatical to work on the Neasden project, finding the right stone.

Then putting it in the right place.

The Abu Dhabi temple will have a façade of pink stone, and the carvings inside would be made from Aqua Bianca, a special Italian marble. This 'white water' grade of marble features a predominantly white or off-white background colour. The base colour may vary slightly, ranging from pure white to creamy tones. What sets Aqua Bianca marble apart is its intricate veining patterns, which can be delicate or bold. The veins can appear in various shades of grey, blue, or even light brown, creating a visually stunning and dynamic surface. Marble may be cold, but people like Sagoon warm it and make it come alive with their passion and their love.

Indeed, he is a happy man. And his garden will just have to wait.

An Electric Man

Ullas Shukla, a quiet man in a quiet place, keeps tabs on twenty-nine separate facilities at the mandir site; be they mechanical, electrical or intricate plumbing. His enthusiasm is infectious. For forty years a corporate man, this former vice president of the Reliance Group could now be enjoying a hard-earned retirement. But in September 2021, something happened; an epiphany of sorts. The fates decreed otherwise and through a common friend, he found himself on the hotline, talking to Swami Brahmaviharidas.

The swami asked him to visit Dubai and make a personal assessment of the enterprise and the tasks ahead. 'I would like you to come and see how the work is and then decide how you like it. I don't want you to say yes and then come here only to realize that you do not like it,' Swami said. In Swami Brahmaviharidas speak, that was translated as, 'I know you will be in raptures and will love the challenge, and you will join up.'

Sure enough, a quick visit to the UAE and the next thing you know, Reliance was about to lose its senior vice president.

The magnitude of the construction does not faze him, having handled mega projects for the Group. It is the spiritual pursuit that is of essence. 'Mahant Swami Maharaj said that this project will be ready on time. Everyone will do the work with unity because it is truly blessed.'

From Motels to Mandirs

All good things come in threes. So too, the directors of the Abu Dhabi Mandir. Madhusudan Patel worked as an engineer in London for nearly three decades. He had heard a temple was being built in Neasden, and through his friendship with Sagoon and an introduction to Swami Brahmaviharidas, found himself involved in a search for the right place to build the mandir. A place in Harrow had been designated but it fell through, and so the hunt continued.

It was a high-prestige exercise because this was the first mandir of such magnitude to be constructed and so no stone could be left unturned, whether in getting the best materials, structural integrity in design and yes, the stone itself. During visits to India to study firsthand how the domes and shikhars would work, his concentration was focused on research and more research. Several famous mandirs in India were scrutinized and data was collected. Then there were local council laws in the UK, and the findings and ideas gleaned from the Indian tour had to comply with them before they could be implemented.

With the three musketeers, Sagoon, Madhu and Ullas, on the same page and working as a unit, it came as no surprise that by February 2024, the Abu Dhabi mandir was ready to welcome the world.

Adil Keeps the Ship in Safe Waters

One day, we were sitting around chewing the fat and discussing a title for the book when someone mentioned Adil Ali. We were scheduled to have an unusual chat with an unusual man.

Ali is a lawyer of good standing, a man of solid fibre and the person who has kept the good ship of BAPS on the right course and steered it away from all the shoals and coral reefs at every step of the way, right from the day the construction of the temple became a reality.

Ali is also an Emirati. This gives him a 360-degree view of things and his advice is both priceless and relevant.

So, what is an Emirati lawyer doing being so involved with a bunch of Hindu monks? What can they possibly have in common? I am watching them interact and they are so comfortable with each other. The journalist in me is intrigued by this relationship because it comes off as unusually friendly and intimate.

Ali is so clear in his mind about what brought them close. It all began when the former President of India Dr A.P.J. Abdul Kalam visited the UAE. There was a function, and Ali was present. Until this point, he had no inkling of what was to come. It was on a Friday that Ali first met Swami Brahmaviharidas. They kind of clicked, and Ali was introduced to some of the other sadhus. Their camaraderie and the ease with which they included him in the general conversation obviously left an impression on him: 'I did not know who they were or what they stood for. But their harmony, the comfortable atmosphere and the intellectual stimulation were endearing. They seemed so keen to learn from each other, and there was no arrogance or any hidden agenda. When I realized these people were exactly what you saw and so transparent, I became a little more involved. The relationship grew, and what caught my interest was the flow of knowledge. You sit with Swami Brahmaviharidas, and you learn so much on so many different topics.'

Run Silent Run Deep

If I owned thirty-one ships, I might have been insufferable. Maybe not. Even one ship could have turned my head. But every now and then, you come across someone so genuine that it hurts—even if he had a fleet of ships and a fleet of Hawker 4000 jets, this man would march to his own drumbeat and keep such a low profile that most people would not hear of him. Clearly, he loves it that way.

With the higher purpose of 'delivering prosperity to humanity' as the core value of his business and life, Ramesh is a person passionately driven by his mission.

With good, solid business sense, oriented to the nuclear family and his larger family of employees, there is a gleam of deep-seated wisdom in his eyes.

That he is held in great esteem and affection by his team is evident from the fact that there are no mental trumpets playing because the chairman is walking in the corridors. No one has to skid out of his way or duck him; an ease which is very telling. I notice it straight away. He is approachable for anyone in the organization and has an open-door policy. They love Ramesh Ramakrishnan and what he stands for. His office in Jebel Ali is like him: efficient, no-frills, pleasantly minimalist and dedicated to being functional, with an aura of positivity and mutual respect.

He refers to the person serving tea as '*beta*', and you know then and there, this is a lot of all right.

Arriving in the UAE circa 1989, this shipping magnate has transformed Transworld into a major player on the high seas as a leading shipping and logistics group. We share a few facts in common: at that time, neither he nor I had ever heard of the Swaminarayan mission. We were both impressed by Swami Brahmaviharidas and his soothing counsel. We are not overly religious, but we are God-fearing and try to be kind and fair in our dealings.

During the COVID-19 pandemic, Ramesh worked closely with BAPS in transporting oxygen cylinders from Dubai on Transworld ships to hospitals and medical centres. He recounts how he had always felt that a temple project of this magnitude in the UAE was deserving, seeing how the population graph showed a large contingent of believers who needed a place to go to seek and find spiritual comfort. His take is very interesting. With such a haven to go to, the large workforce will gravitate there for some religious and learning communion and not engage in less attractive pastimes and activities on a Sunday.

'Crime, petty conflict, self-indulgence with alcohol—all these will become secondary,' he says. A sublimity will be induced in people.

He lauds the support given by the UAE leadership and how it has not just espoused this enterprise but actually got involved in its progress. He harkens back to 1997 and the moment at dusk on the sands of Sharjah, when Pramukh Swami prayed that one day there would be this temple of a thousand years.

'The more I met these people, the more I was taken in by their work ethic. They were so different from the image we have of holy people. This movement seems to attract intellect as well as devotion, both being the elements reflected in the temple initiative. A place to pray and a place to learn.'

The more Ramesh spent time in their midst, the more enamoured he became by what you can only term the high efficiency of BAPS, the need to get results with minimum fuss and the value for time. Every minute must count, so they do not squander it. Swami Brahmaviharidas's boundless energy and the amount of work accomplished in a twenty-four-hour cycle was impressive, indeed.

Ramesh wanted to do something for the awesome enterprise. The equation formed itself.

'Their whole accent was on delivering the promise, and their system, to me, seemed flawless. They have so much positive energy.' He points to young Yogi Bhatt, the official aide to Swami Brahmaviharidas. 'This young man is the perfect example of the BAPS approach to work. He never says no, gets things done without fuss and networks with so much rapport; it's a perfect combination.'

Ramesh runs more than just a tight ship and to be so successful, he demands the same qualities in his rank and file. This relationship intensified over the days of delivery, and today, there is a genuine bond of mutual respect between Transworld and the BAPS mission.

'With every meeting, I came out feeling good, spiritually elevated. That is how I decided that I was getting tangible satisfaction out of our relationship, so I must give something back.

'I heard that much of the materials for building the temple were being brought from India, and it was a fair amount. I cannot hazard a guess, but it was substantial. There was sandstone from Rajasthan and other parts of the world, and there were thousands of intricately carved figures of deities and sacred animals sculpted by 2,000 artisans in a place called Pindwara, and all of it had to be shipped.

'I had the ships.

'The fact that COVID-19 had upped the costs of cargo by 1,500 per cent did not deter me. I would absorb the costs and offer the space gratis. My teams on both ends echoed the enthusiasm. They saw this opportunity as a service and a blessing that they had been granted by the grace of God. We designed the pallets with tender care to ensure maximum protection for the fragile carvings.'

I interrupt him. I say I have it from a good source that 20,000 tonnes of materials have been shipped, and there has been no breakage. That is astounding, even with special care; this has to be some divine intervention that has put loss at zero.

He agrees, says his staff feels the same way. 'They are delighted with being given the task; they have taken the responsibility upon themselves.'

My partner in crime, Umeshchandran Raja, an eminent educationalist in the UK and currently a volunteer at the mission, helping with the media end of things, asks Ramesh if just handling these religious figurines had a salutary impact on the staff. Ramesh says, 'Oh yes, indeed, it became a mission and a challenge as we transported pallet after pallet, each with great care.

'They felt it was beyond duty; it was a calling, and you could see that day and night became one as our ships were loaded in such a way that there was no pressure on these sections. I have to say the enormous support in India and the UAE was unprecedented. At both ends, whether it was Customs or Immigration or any other authority, the support was exemplary. This incredible cooperation and the astute handling of every shipment at the site ensured that everything arrived intact.'

He says he feels a surge of satisfaction, almost an emotional surrender, whenever he visits the site and observes the progress.

'It is coming up beautifully and on schedule, and I will say I am so grateful for this opportunity I was given to be of a little help and be a part of this historical spiritual edifice.'

It is typical of the man that he underplays the importance of his contribution. 'Little' does not even begin to describe it.

Generosity and Godliness

Thirty years and more. It has been a long time. But the ravages of age seem to have slipped past Yogesh Mehta. I am sitting in his office, and he still has that very engaging smile. Trim and fit, clearly belying his years. We used to exchange greetings and pleasantries from way back in the '90s, as we gravitated on the outer rim of the expat social orbit. In candid confession, on those occasions, I spent more time with his delightful wife, Falguni. She would occasionally send me comments on my articles in the newspapers—and who in this world does not like flattery?

I would hear about her husband's success with Petrochem through the grapevine and how he had built it into a company to reckon with, but I didn't know much more. Piety, to be honest, was not something that fought for a link with Yogesh. The family prayed and venerated, but life was still on the fast track. In Dadar, Mumbai, his elders had been very close to Yogiji Maharaj and sought his counsel on many occasions. In fact, Yogesh was named after Yogiji, and it was plain deference that called for a subtle change in his official nomenclature to make Yogi into Yogesh.

Now, as we sit and talk one July afternoon in his gracefully appointed office in Dubai's Jumeirah Lake Towers (JLT) complex, I have to admit he has taken God, generosity and golf and turned them into the three legs of a tripod on which he so successfully balances his day-to-day life. Generosity from folks like him was something that used to be talked about on the circuit, but never set to music. His golf has improved from enthusiasm to more skill (though no less enthusiastic), and he addresses that little white ball (one of which is nestled on his table) with the same attention and acuity as he does his role in the BAPS commitment to building a mandir in the Emirates.

That faith and godliness go back many generations. His great grandfather was a great believer and so the Swaminarayan way of life was absorbed at an early age. A fifth-generation fealty continues the devotion, as he and his son, Rohan, continue to display deference. When Yogesh heard that this grand gesture of making a major temple was a reality, he knew he had to find a role for himself. For some time, he had been meaning to meet Swami Brahmaviharidas, but as with most good intentions, it just had not panned out. One or the other was always out of town.

Then, one day, around 2016, Yogesh heard that Swamiji was in town and had been sending emissaries out to find this elusive Yogesh Mehta.

'So, what I did was ask Rohan to accompany me. Let's finally go call on Swami in the house at Jaffiliya. We had sent a message that we were coming, so we were expected. When we entered, Swamiji was holding court, but when he saw me, he was especially warm and welcoming.'

The two clicked instantly and their conversation was as crisp as French fries.

'You cannot help but fall under the happy spell of Swamiji's intellect and wisdom and the way he imparts it. He is ready for your argument and welcomes it, but it must make sense for him to accept it. For me, every meeting after that has been a blessing; I just come away feeling like my batteries have been recharged.'

Yogesh recalls that afternoon clearly. Suddenly, with no planning whatsoever, he extended an invitation to Swamiji. 'It just came out. I said, "You are going to come to my home, bless it and stay with us".

'Swamiji smiled that gentle signature smile and said, "Yes, I will surely come."

'"Not just visit, Swamiji, I want you to stay with me, in my home."'

Yogesh says he did keep his promise and spent five days with him. 'It was a joyous and learning experience.'

Today, Yogesh is a major pillar on the BAPS board for this mandir as a vice chairman, trustee and what he calls himself: 'an ambassador of goodwill'.

'I am in awe of this project, and I do believe that the government has honoured our community and sent out a stentorian message of interfaith tolerance and harmony. I hope this sort of message is echoed all over the world.'

Praising the UAE leaders and seeing that this house of worship will also be a house of learning and recognition for all faiths and civilizations, gives Yogesh a deep sense of fulfilment.

'Part of my obligations call for seeking funding and contributions from those who can afford it. It does surprise me that generosity can come from the oddest places. And yet, from where you think it might or must or should, the purse strings stay closed. This is such a good cause, you are contributing to an institution, to a future, to an iconic edifice, and you cannot find it in you to step forward. Fortunately, there are only a few such people, and I have never understood the absence of largesse, not just in money, but in giving time also.'

Dismay does not play a big part. Every day is a new day with new challenges, and like the game of golf he loves so much, he knows one cannot decide the lay of the ball, only what club to use at every stroke, designed for maximum benefit.

Wonder Women

If there is one area that is misunderstood or at least often misinterpreted, it is the belief that women are somewhat sidelined and secondary to all BAPS proceedings, almost being ostracized. Nothing could be further from the truth. Women have a very prominent role, and truth be told, they constitute over 60 per cent of the followers. Because the swamis have taken a spiritual vow of celibacy as part of their austerity pledge, their distancing is often misunderstood. The irony is that the women themselves feel no such isolation and revel in their roles.

One afternoon, I found myself with a group of ladies who happily answered some deeper questions I had about the role of women in BAPS.

After a meaningful conversation with them, a few things became evident. The women in the BAPS ranks make pivotal contributions to spiritual development, community service and the preservation of cultural and religious heritage.

In fact, it was a progressive Bhagwan Swaminarayan who called for an end to *sati* and *dudhpiti*—the killing of female babies—half a century before the passing of Female Infanticide Prevention Act, 1870. In addition, he advocated and promoted the education of rural women far before it was common practice anywhere in India and perhaps anywhere in the world.

His teachings have given women a spur to be active and thousands of them firmly believe that love for the guru transcends the absurd notion of gender bias.

In BAPS, women equally engage in daily spiritual practices, such as prayers, meditation and the study of sacred texts. By the same token, women are dynamic contributors to diverse forms of community service and volunteer work. They also have important roles in the education and upbringing of the younger generation, transmitting religious and cultural knowledge. BAPS has integrated women into administrative and leadership positions of great global impact—dare I say in a more genuine way than many other more 'progressive' organizations you see in the world.

Armed with this knowledge, I talk to the six ladies, and this is what they say in capsule.

Meet Sapna Manish Dipikar, a functional consultant. She is tasked with handling satsang activities and administration as well as 'engaging' people in different jobs.

Shaily Pranav Desai is an academician and at no stage sees herself as second-class. On the contrary, she feels truly blessed to be found worthy of service.

Vijayshree Guha is a planning manager and brings her forte to bear on organizing a range of events; she is categorical: 'Our love for our guru makes us equal to everyone, because he does not see us as any less.'

Binita Sagar is an administrator at the mandir, overseeing many departments, such as transport, security and facilities. Without getting paid one cent, one might ask what benefit does she derive? 'Satisfaction. I am purifying my soul. I am always available to help out, and the opportunities empower me. Gender discrimination? Wouldn't be here if there was.'

Chanda Pagrani is a partner in a real estate company of high repute and says to me: 'Spiritual love is not blind; it helps you see farther and deeper. We are content, and we love doing the seva we do.' She has to be for real and mean every word she says, because it would be easy for her and all the others to get on the bling mill and live a life of self-indulgent luxury if they wished to.

I have also had the privilege of meeting Sonali Chirayu Patel on several occasions. Her confidence and eloquence speak for themselves. She projects herself as a mother and wife, but she is one of the major motivators in the BAPS UAE organization and someone people admire.

These are all women of substance, multitasking in life while still having the time and energy to engage in good work. Not only do they successfully debunk the concept that women are secondary in the sanstha, they also clarify that what is seen as 'disrespect' by certain ignorant quarters, is actually a deep and abiding respect for women. In fact, in return, they honour the oaths and pledges and commitment of the swamis to a certain spartan way of life.

I, for one, will buy into that with no qualms whatsoever.

River of Giving

Every now and again, I do a little good or, as Paul Eddington of *Yes Minister* fame once said, 'I do very little harm.' I pay off school fees, clear someone's small medical bill, give an ice cream treat to street kids in India; little things that stroke the ego and hopefully bring a smile to a face that has little to smile about. Then, I meet someone like Manish Patel and realize there is a lot of 'good and decent' out there. A lot more of this 'quiet tribe' than gets credit.

Manish volunteered to be of service to BAPS set up in the UAE and ensure their sustenance. The sadhus, the staff, the volunteers, the workers, everyone connected to the construction of the temple in Abu Dhabi, is offered catering by the Manish Corporation. Now, you might say, okay, what is so special about the arrangement? There is no bill. He does not charge for dry rations, groceries, fresh foods, juices, tea, coffee, water, delivery, overheads—all these are absorbed by the parent company.

The Last Word . . . Belief Is a Rock

The last word goes to the miracle. This book was first entitled '101 Miracles'. With good cause. As it picked up its own speed and direction—as books tend to do when there is no fixed agenda—the dynamics changed. But one miracle stands out. And it is best described by David Light, a journalist at *Khaleej Times*, where I was the editor:

'Where we stood during the test, the profile of the rock actually isn't flat. The profile is like we are standing on the backbone of something, because of its sloped down surface; it's something like a backbone, which immediately triggered the thought of an elephant. We have such a big "bone" to support the Mandir,' said Dr Keong, SOE Consultants' executive director.

'I am very honoured to be part of this team because this is the first time doing a project that would last a minimum of 1,000 years,' he added.

Sandeep Vyas, principal civil engineer, Air Products, said the initial geotechnical survey showed a 20-metre thick stone in the centre of the plot where the Mandir was expected to be built.

'We found competent bedrock very close to the existing ground level,' Vasiahmed Behlim, lead structural engineer, RSP, added.

Tinu Simon, Project Manager, Shapoorji Pallonji, said, 'When we started this project, I was really surprised because before reaching the excavation level itself, we reached high rock. More than 15 years I am working in the GCC, and for the first time, I found such a good foundation within such limit.'

Talking about the design of a 1,000-year foundation, Sanjay Parikh, Planning Cell, BAPS, pointed out, 'This will be a totally un-reinforced structure and will not have any ferrous metals used, as per our ancient Shilpa Shastra.'

Fly ash has been used to fill up the foundation, thereby replacing 55 per cent of the cement in the concrete mix, making it eco-friendly and reducing its carbon footprint.*

See you in 3024.

---

* Ashwani Kumar, 'UAE: Abu Dhabi's Hindu temple to last over 1,000 years' (from the *8@8 with David Light* podcast), *Khaleej Times*, 27 September 2021. Available at: https://www.khaleejtimes.com/uae/uae-abu-dhabis-hindu-temple-to-last-over-1000-years.

24

The Moment of Truth

'Let the world have peace and harmony, that is what I pray for every day.'

—*Mahant Swami Maharaj*

The final chapter. The cherry on the cake. There are two ways to handle it. Go straight for the core or pull back a little and ruminate how you got to this point. Does the past throw indicators or is everything random and disconnected?

The way I see it, life is a series of links—a few of them, if you are fortunate, are golden and memorable by the sheer virtue of the personages you meet. The question then is singular: is there a pattern to everyone's life, one that repeats itself even if you don't register this aspect? Events of yesterday prodding you towards the next milestones, signposts clearly marked for you?

So, I consciously probe my life and its intrinsic connections to try and find that elusive pattern, the rare moments, those unique crossings.

One such occasion was when I was invited by the de Klerk government to meet Nelson Mandela, who had been released from Robben Island after twenty-seven years. I recall the African National Congress (ANC) at the time was hugely sensitive and suspicious of all white-oriented initiatives and an Indian journalist from Dubai invited by an apartheid regime was not their idea of a breakthrough. Their reps thwarted any moves to get that meeting. We even drove to Soweto (southwest townships) to Winnie Mandela's house and to Desmond Tutu's but got no joy.

It was just fortuitous that after four fruitless days of trailing him across the country, I dived into an empty hotel pool in Cape Town. Bemused but happy to be alone and splashing, I suddenly realized I had left my watch on the room table and my wallet in an open bag. The hotel had warned us against theft; so uneasily, I got out and made for the elevator.

It dinged, I got in and a gentle soon-to-be-globally-famous voice softly asked if I had enjoyed the swim.

It was the man himself. His security had mishandled the programming of the lift and it had stopped where it wasn't supposed to.

The pleasures of being a journalist, you learn fast, are that when the fates are feeling fondly, you grab the opportunity with both hands. I went for it, told him how no one was letting me meet him; the security glowered, the ANC representatives shuffled their feet and one even looked like he would volunteer most cheerfully to throttle me, when Mr Mandela apologized and said, 'They are new to the job and a little enthusiastic, yes. Let's sit in the tea room and talk.'

What a wonderfully gracious way of admonishing someone. The gentle way, the art of controlling the situation by apologizing and rendering space without losing anything . . .

And since this book is about the Swaminarayan devotees, isn't this uncannily their philosophy, too?

It's been thirty years, but the memory of an extraordinary man having an extraordinary life and never giving up an inch to adversity does leave you impacted; a memory that will never fade.

In a writer's career, celebrities abound and often, the writer erroneously thinks his felicity with words and language entitle him to that status. Not so. A writer is an observer and a chronicler and only once, in a rare way, can he feel he has been hit by a human meteor and granted the beneficence of an audience.

Nelson Mandela was one such golden milestone in my journey. In political terms, Indira Gandhi, Margaret Thatcher and J.R.D. Tata were a notable few others. In terms of the armed forces, meeting Air Chief Marshal P.C. Lal after the 1971 war, and being mute witness to Admiral S.M. Nanda crumbling with grief when he received the flimsy confirming the INS Khukri had been sunk in the same war. And in terms of aviation, the hunt for the wreckage of Air India Flight 855 on New Year's Day 1978 off the Bandra Mumbai Coast and consoling the grief-stricken gathered on the shore, are moments in storytelling that stand out. Realizing how fragile life is, any minute passed with nothing to show for it is a minute squandered.

Then, one day in office, as I was planning a weekend, out of the blue, I was ordered to go with the army cadets of the National Defence Academy to a height of 24,000 feet—in elevation terms a major promotion from buying ice cream on The Mall in Shimla.

The target is Nun Kun at 25,700 feet, and I, an accidental mountaineer. Forty days of unremitting misery earned me the honour of dinner with the legendary Tenzing Norgay, a day when he pinned a Himalayan Mountaineering Institute miniature pickaxe on my lapel.

On that original Everest expedition, I have a take.

I grab my theory and run with it, casting civility aside for a story by being intrusive. I run it again on the cinemascope of my mind. I am doing this while sitting next to Tenzing. On that day, 29 May 1953, Queen Elizabeth II would ascend the throne in far-off London. On the peak of an empire's crumbling wreck, an Englishman would stand on the top of the world. A then lowly Sherpa would not even get an also-ran mention until para nine, that says he was hanging around 8 feet below the summit.

But was he? Would that sinewy, hard-as-rock, tough, natural-born mountain native not have gone up first to check on the safety parameters of where man had never been before and then helped the *sahib* up?

By the same token, though, the Edmund Hillary legend is that of an honourable man—the Livingstone type, adventurous, trailblazing move over Attenborough genre, courage under fire, rode the 500 into the valley of death, a musketeer, gutsy as legless Air ace Douglas Bader, a veritable Jim Corbett with a tiger in his tank, powerful legacies all. He could have taken the lead and gone up first and then pulled his porter to take the famous selfie of the times.

The movie in my mind runs out of reel. So, I ask Tenzing the obvious: who reached up there first, you or Sir Edmund?

We are still on the first course of dinner. He pretends he hasn't heard me. I repeat the question. He laughs as he must have a thousand times and says, 'Only God knows.'

Only God knows. Two men from vastly different backgrounds together on top of the world, looking down on creation and making a solemn promise without even saying it.

Pure harmony, in-sync, oneness of thought, 'We are in this together, no one shall know because it does not matter, we cooperated with each other, we went to the summit as a team, peace to the world and a salute for intruding on the abode of the Gods.'

For a year now, these are exactly the sentiments that mark the rules of conduct of the dramatis personae of this book.

Many years later, on 9 December 2023, I am in the town of Nadiad, a two-hour dusty trip from Ahmedabad. This business hub is home for a few days to Mahant Swami, the sixth spiritual head of the BAPS Swaminarayan Sanstha and the direct successor to Pramukh Swami, whose centenary was celebrated in Ahmedabad for a glorious month in 2022–23.

'Only God knows' will echo as a sentiment once again here, but on that day, I didn't know that. All I did know is that sitting in the hotel room in Ahmedabad, I was practising protocol based on little nuggets of information gleaned from BAPS volunteers and the inimitable Swami Brahmaviharidas, whose mission it is to embarrass me with praise and tease me about my unformed and skinny spiritual prowess—more the lack of it.

I was scheduled to meet Mahant Swami, the spiritual head of BAPS and a man so venerated and loved that even a five-second audience with him is considered a benediction. I had no idea what to expect, but I wanted to be on cue. This was the first holy man of such stature that I was hoping to interview, and I was nervous about how it would go.

So, I was practising. To do the right thing. I don't bend and touch feet, because it wasn't taught to me. As a gesture, it is so wonderfully Indian and gracious to the core, but it has to have a graceful and natural contour, and I was not sure I could carry it off. Besides much confusion, since I am left-handed, I didn't know if a left-handed swoop is acceptable or a gaffe; I prayed somebody would tell me the protocol.

I was also practising the cadence of the questions with a Plan A and a Plan B. There is a method to the practice. You rehearse and then act as if it's all extempore and off-the-cuff. And you make a powerful impression on your audience, because you stood in front of that mirror and worked at it. I have never believed there is anything like communicating off the top of your head spontaneously, when addressing an august audience.

So, I was working on my drill to make sure I got it right. I bet even Mark Anthony quickly scooted to a corner and did a few quick runs of the 'Friends, Romans, and Countrymen' speech before delivering it at Caesar's funeral. All speakers, great and small, they must work at being eloquent.

And as we drive into the temple premises, the sense of spirituality intensifies in subtle increments. I'd never seen so many swamis in one place. There is in equal measure a carnival-like lightness, and everyone seems so cheerful. Between the thousands of visitors and the BAPS swamis in saffron, there is an inescapable camaraderie. I ask why so many people have gathered, like over 5,000. I am told they have come to see Pujya Mahant Swami, because he will be giving darshan today. He was also going to bless a marriage today, which is very rare and definitely one for the books. We are invited to the ceremony, where we join in the chanting and the prayers, but then we learn that we have to undergo a COVID-19 swab test before a personal audience with Mahant Swami.

So, we leave the ceremony prematurely, little realizing that we are risking missing a momentous occasion where the sixth spiritual successor of Bhagwan Swaminarayan was actually blessing a wedding ceremony.

We now enter a large room that serves as the COVID-19 test area and also stands in as an annex to the swami's residence. Swabbed and stressing as we wait for the results, we watch a group of smart young men setting the room up for the interview.

They are again the ubiquitous volunteers who appear like genies from a bottle, giving up their holiday time to be of service. As an onlooker over the year, this flow of good people doing good things on their dime and asking for no compensation continues to astound me. They should be oversleeping, going on a date, watching a cricket match, engaging in that splendid Indian label of 'time pass'—a great way of squandering the seconds. Yet here they are, wanting to be of worth. I never tire of arrowing the same question at them, hoping that the sharp bolt will elicit some fresh reply like, 'It is a penance for our sins, hence the service,' or something else I can peg to logic because the consistency of the selflessness is neither easy to digest nor understand. The cynicism of the journalist wants a more prosaic explanation; a flaw rooted in human frailty, at least some guilt for some misdeeds.

Even as I provoke and probe, I get the same answer about how happy everyone is to be working for the pleasure of serving Bhagwan Swaminarayan, the COVID-19 test results come in.

We are good to go. But we cannot go. We have to stay in temporary isolation because this is where we will meet Mahant Swami. So, we miss the wedding blessings and the extraordinary rituals which have been performed. More is the pity.

Minutes later, the action starts. Swamis in an assortment of shapes and sizes yet so dressed in identical saffron that there is a visual sameness, and it begins to exude a certain urgency.

It is akin to an orchestra warming up for its magnum opus.

The anticipation mercury climbs swiftly, and you can sense the dynamics of the room changing from ho-hum to a palpable but happy tension.

There are no drums or clarion calls but amazingly, you hear them in your ears from some inner source; a dryness in the mouth, a nervous licking of lips—like it is finally happening, whatever it is. The swarm of swamis present are sending semaphoric signals on the progress of Mahant Swami and how far he is from arrival. It is an amazing sensation, these last few seconds before the big moment. You are excited, little stabs of panic assail you, the impact of where you are and the privilege of being in this presence paradoxically prod you to consider escape, like 'what am I doing here, what if Mahant Swami sees through me and says, "You have brought me here at 9.30 p.m. to meet *this* imposter?! I have better things to do, this guy is not sincere, not spiritual enough, you should vet people before bringing them to me."'

The previous night, my imagination had run wild well past 2 a.m.; I was sleep talking: 'Do I address him as Your Holiness, call him Swamiji, stand and talk, can we sit in a chair or does it have to be on the floor, what if I get a back spasm without a backrest, a coughing fit, anything clumsy and oafish . . .'

The night ended. The sun came out. This was it. We were here.

Feelings broiling, the heart racing in response to the sheer power of the moment, and then he enters, helped by two disciples, but holding his own as he walks in and is made comfortable.

Give me a minute to digress here. Every now and then, you meet someone whose radiance actually emanates from their countenance like ultraviolet rays; so natural that no cosmetic can achieve such effect, however expensive. It is like someone has switched on a light from within them. I have tried to figure out the magical reason. But nothing definitive. A mix of things. Maybe they know some great celestial secret we don't. Perhaps the complete lack of interest in material pursuits provides a wonderful sense of freedom. Prayer and meditation inch them closer to the Almighty, hence the glow. An inner peace, their humours in harmony. But it is there—soft and gentle, almost captivating in its brilliance.

Swami Brahmaviharidas is introducing me, and I am trying not to stare; all I can think at that moment is 'goodness, he exists, he is not just a photograph, he is smiling at me and now there is a silence, and he is waiting patiently for me to ask my first question.'

I say, 'My children asked me to ask you this question: you inspire millions, they look up to you for guidance and spiritual comfort; who inspires you?'

He spreads his hands as if to say, ah, that is an easy one.

And then he says, 'God. God knows, only God.'

Tenzing Norgay, where are you? There you are . . . the same answer. The connection is stark; my theory of links is strengthened even further.

I further probed, 'Then, who inspires you here on this earth?'

He says, 'My Guru Pramukh Swami Maharaj.'

There are four of us facing Mahant Swami. Seated next to him is Swami Brahmaviharidas acting as facilitator, coordinator, translator and catalyst for having made this meeting possible and choreographing its success. My co-editors, British educationalist Umesh Raja and young Hari Patel, have both worked on the book and with them, businessman Tusharbhai forms the panel, but they all defer to me graciously in asking the questions.

I mention the readiness of the mandir in Abu Dhabi and ask Mahant Swami how he thinks Pramukh Swami would have felt seeing his 1997 prophecy approaching the realm of reality.

He spreads his hands in a fulsome and spontaneous gesture, his expression brightening even more, if possible, as if the Oracle had spoken.

Clearly, he would be ecstatic. And why not? Nearly thirty years after the prediction that practically no one believed, it was all coming so marvellously true.

This brings me to the crux of my question campaign. In December 2020, Mahant Swami wrote a letter to Swami Brahmaviharidas, and it is a classic in itself. The world was in turmoil, COVID-19 had us all in an evil thrall; families were hurting, no one knew what tomorrow would bring, or if there would even be a tomorrow. The letter says so much so eloquently, and if you can read between the lines, you will see that there is that unshakeable conviction that there will be an end to the turmoil. A good end. A resolution at the end of a dark and forbidding tunnel.

This letter is, therefore, worth sharing with the world.

* * *

Swami Shriji
Param Pujya Pramukh Swami
Nenpur 22/12/20
Tuesday, Magshar Sud 8

To Pujya Brahmavihari Swami, who has been immensely graced by Pramukh Swami Maharaj,

Heartiest Jay Swaminarayan and with great love from Sadhu Keshavjivandas.

Today is the ninety-ninth birth celebration anniversary of Param Pujya Pramukh Swami Maharaj.

Pramukh Swami has silently completed many great deeds whilst living amongst us.

No pretence whatsoever, that's it! He did everything only to please and fulfil the wishes of Shastriji Maharaj and Yogiji Maharaj.

In the same way, we too must fulfil the divine wishes of Pramukh Swami and greatly please him.

As you mentioned, in 1997, in the desert of Sharjah, Pramukh Swami Maharaj prayed:

'May peace prevail here and everywhere in the world, may the religions of each country grow in mutual love, may each country be freed from prejudices towards each other and progress in their own way.' Alongside this, Pramukh Swami Maharaj also made a divine wish that a mandir will be built in Abu Dhabi.

That wish is being fulfilled today.

In this way, we have prayed for years for peace to prevail in the Gulf countries.

And due to the grace of God, a mandir is being constructed in Abu Dhabi today.

This is God's doing.

It is taking shape with everyone's support and cooperation. The revered Crown Prince of Abu Dhabi, Sheikh Mohammed bin Zayed Al Nahyan, has generously gifted us a vast stretch of land, a gesture attributed to the influence and bond shared with our esteemed Prime Minister of India, Shri Narendra Modi. Till the sun and moon shine!

Upon this, a mandir with seven spires will be erected, where the avatars (incarnations) of God will be ceremoniously consecrated.

Alongside being a Hindu place of worship, it will be a beautiful complex of harmony.

This is not merely a mandir made of stones and bricks, but it will be a mandir of love, peace and harmony.

For such a mandir and such sacred images to be erected in this country is a miracle.

Miracle! Nobody can even imagine it.

Spiritual leaders, esteemed guests and visitors that I meet, all say that this is a miracle, a new chapter in history, a new era.

I myself cannot understand how everything has fallen into place, my mind cannot comprehend. It is a heaven in the desert, the power of God.

Out of all the mandirs thus far, this mandir will be the best.

It will be the pinnacle of spirituality.

Prayers that have been said for hundreds of years by our ancestors for a mandir to be built in UAE will come to fruition.

The tales of India's rich culture will be carved.

Unity, fraternity and solidarity are the virtues of God.

The souls of everyone in the universe will be drawn here.

Well-wishers from all countries will come here to do darshan.

It will become a spiritual oasis of global harmony from which interfaith harmony, community cohesion, righteous living and international friendship will flourish.

You will get everyone's support for this divine wish of Pramukh Swami.

The King will be the preserver. HH Sheikh Abdullah and HH Sheikh Nahyan will support. Both will offer support. The ambassadors and officials of the UAE will assist as if it is their own.

In this sanctuary of solidarity, support will pour in from all four directions. Even in ways we have never imagined or comprehended, support will arrive unexpectedly. Every religion will offer its support, considering this cause to be their own.

People of all ages, from the youngest to the eldest, will wholeheartedly engage in seva, devoting themselves entirely to this cause. The young and the old will be the keepers of this mandir, ensuring its continuity. Even the deities themselves will partake in this seva. We have experienced this firsthand. How do we convey this phenomenon to others?

This temple will be an abode of Indian culture, civilization and values. The bells of humanity will resound across the world.

Not just on the Moon, not just on Mars, but it will resonate throughout the entire universe. This temple will become globally renowned.

Bells of solidarity and unity will ring. Solidarity and unity are prevailing in all four directions. Love, peace and harmony are in the atmosphere. It's felt in everyone's heart.

I can see this before my own eyes. If you divide this land into a hundred parts, a miracle will occur in every part. There will be a succession of miracles. Miracles that will transform hearts and change lives.

Unimaginable good works will happen. The impossible will become possible.

The BAPS Hindu Mandir in Abu Dhabi will be a haven of unity, support, culture and civilization.

A new era will dawn.

Jay Shri Swaminarayan.

* * *

The letter itself offers so many answers that my questionnaire shrinks dramatically. But I soldier on with more questions.

'Is there a message for the rulers and the government of the UAE from you about this unique Mandir?'

Mahant Swami replies, 'I wish them peace and harmony. We are grateful recipients of their largesse and sense of tolerance, a perfect example to the rest of the world of how to generate togetherness and show a deep and abiding love for mankind. This mandir symbolizes all that is good in our world and will offer millions hope, calm, kindness and a sense of caring for each other.

'This is a great nation with an enlightened leadership, and we will always be grateful.

'Yes, the one way we can achieve these values is to give respect to gain respect and make this mandir as much a house of learning as it is a house of worship and an oasis for every faith.'

Mahant Swami demands peace for humanity with a certain conviction that it is globally reachable if we all work, live and believe together.

Like Pramukh Swami had prophesied the building of the mandir as far back as 1997, Mahant Swami had indicated with great foresight the arrival of goodwill ambassadors to the site of the mandir in his letter of 2020.

On 26 May 2023, in an unprecedented move that would have made the UN proud, as many as thirty envoys from that many nations and their families spent a very special day at the site and inadvertently gave credence to Mahant Swami's prediction of bonding: 'They will come from far and carry back with them the message of peace and harmony and above all the power of prayer.'

In a gist, through the conversation, the many splendoured interpretations of God given by the Swami can be captured:

- All is ordained, and God decides what will be done.
- Prayer is a mandate and service to others, a calling of the highest order.
- Peace is not elusive if we actively seek it.
- Love for God is all the inspiration that man needs.
- Devotion to God becomes a beautiful duty.
- In essence, do right and the right will happen.

Mahant Swami smiles with a warmth that drives away any chill in the room. He blesses the first edition of the book.

He says something about me to Swami Brahmaviharidas, but it is said with affection, and I know I have not been labelled an imposter, so I do not press for a translation.

Relief is significant and then Mahant Swami beckons me towards him. Since we were advised to maintain a bit of distance, I somewhat hesitate and pull back.

'He wants you to hold his hand in yours,' says Swami Brahmaviharidas.

I am still not sure, so I am tentative.

'Well, go on then, take his hand.'

I do that. In a sort of gentle, soft touch, in a 'I don't want to hurt him' fashion.

He looks at me, this ninety-year-old sixth leader of a major religious organization, and he smiles and strengthens his grip. He is now pressing my palm; he does it three times in quick succession and the twinkling in his eyes seems to say, 'God is my strength.'

It suddenly hits me, he is happy, and I feel this wash of humility like, 'Why me, I don't deserve it.'

For a fraction of a second, I feel like the imposter I hope I am not. Then, I say with self-belief, 'Why not me?' and exult in the magic of the moment, both playful and profound.

His entourage is already stunned that he has stayed so long. I might now add, at the lightheartedness of the texture of that past half hour, the disciples now begin to indicate it is time to conclude.

Honest to God, tell me this is pure arrogance on my part, but Mahant Swami would have stayed, we were having such a good time. I daresay he was interested and amused, and for whatever reason, loving the banter between Swami Brahmaviharidas and myself, as well as the elaborate yet cheerful translations being offered by Swami Brahmaviharidas to him.

I am so hugely enjoying being in the presence of this incredible personage that I fall back on some of my favourite lines of poetry. I say, 'The woods are lovely, dark and deep, / But I have promises to keep, / And miles to go before I sleep. Mahant Swami, what promises do you still have to keep?'

He furrows a gentle brow and then says, 'To promote peace, to build harmony, to offer comfort and carry out the wishes of Pramukh Swami at every step.'

What better response. It is crisp, clear and memorable.

They say memory begins to let you down with age, you grapple to recall. Not Mahant Swami. He looks at Umesh Raja when he is being introduced and after a pause, he says, 'You were once on a plane with me, we flew together.'

And it is true. Once, in 2004. It says a lot about his memory, considering he sees thousands of people. Umesh Raja is awed, as are we.

In conclusion, Swami Brahmaviharidas remembered by name all the swamis and volunteers serving at the mandir site.

And then sought special blessings for each one of us sitting before him. Mahant Swami once again glowed and opened his arms and said, 'You all are my family.' His words and gesture were all-embracing.

As we finally rose, Swami Brahmaviharidas asked me if I had any kind of wish to express. To make a sort of fatuous, humorous end note, I said, 'Swamiji, tell my wife to love me more.'

He paused, smiled and said, 'If God wills it.'

I part reluctantly, wanting more. There is a sense of elation and wonderment. Did this really happen? I feel like I am walking on air, almost a mystical cleansing of the soul; with the elation, a certain calm; that keen awareness of having been in a presence . . . as Swami Brahmaviharidas would say, 'Not bad going for someone non-spiritual.'

One last question I should have asked Swamiji, witnessing his depth of insight: was it Tenzing Norgay or Sir Edmund Hillary that reached the summit of Mount Everest first?

And Mahant Swami would have replied, 'Does it matter? They worked together, as a team, a partnership in the best sense, mutual respect, honour, and most importantly for the greater good. Only God knows that the answer is they did it together, because they could not have done it alone.'

And that is the harmony we all seek.

Afterword

'I am that ordinary person.'

—*Bikram Vohra*

Are we the sum of our experiences? If so, why do we exhaust so much energy in denying the influence or fighting against it?

The last one year for me has been quite a journey, writing on the BAPS Swaminarayan Sanstha and the building of a Hindu temple in Abu Dhabi.

Has some of that spirituality rubbed off on me, reworked my wiring, made me a different person?

A better person?

I wasn't too bad to start with, so the improvement would not register on this Richter scale. None of my bad habits and indulgences have sloughed off, and I still worry about my two ends meeting. If there has been some positive fallout from the association in this connection, I guess it is that I am resigned to the two ends not becoming close friends. No lottery ticket has my number on it.

And I am vaguely calmer. I no longer go round yelling about who left the A/C on, you think money grows on trees, what did you pay for this, that's too much, why doesn't anyone listen to good sense? The sad verbal detritus of those who have grown old; their laments seeking some stronghold, a traction to still be counted.

This effort of writing the book gave me that beachhead, and I have felt more relevant at that stage when you fear no one wants your opinion about anything, and you are just whistling in the wind.

Besides making me calmer, it has also been an insightful saga. From gently poking fun without malice at young men and women surrendering *la dolce vita* and the sensual side of heady materialism for ascetic service, I have begun to admire them for their conviction, their steadfastness and the unquestioning love for what they do so willingly. By this very token, I am so blown out of the water by the tsunami of volunteers who give every moment of their time in service and ask for nothing in return. You cannot pretend to be this committed, it has to come from the heart.

So yes, even if you start off the exercise as a professional writer, you cannot help being impacted over the months. With calmness you pick up patience, warmth and caring, a certain endurance for the long haul and a sliver of guilt that for so many years, God has been a shadowy figure of convenience. Met with and fawned upon when floundering in dire straits but for the large part, shunted onto a parallel track and from a distance paid sincere lip service—if that is not an oxymoron.

Not disbelieving, just so many other things to do.

Then the swamis and their value system. Modern in thought yet ascetic, happy yet sans any possessions, not even a watch, glowing with an inner illumination that is very difficult to capture. Men of such intellectual calibre and so accomplished that you are compelled to mind your p's and q's, because their knowledge of up there and why and how is balanced by an acute awareness of here and now in the twenty-first century. From metaphysics to philosophy to politics, some of them would be shoo-ins at Oxford's debating society.

From them, I have learnt a lot. I learnt there are many sides to a prism, that things are ordained for a reason, that love is not a commodity but a way of life, that coming to terms with yourself is a mandate and sharing and giving counsel a duty.

Perhaps the singular lesson imbibed is that no one is too heavy to become a burden; we are all in the same boat and a sense of purpose and intent every minute of every day is the essence of life.

Like with rubber bands that you can stretch and pull and twist, perhaps the novelty will wear off and I will return to my original shape.

But I think not. The impact *has* occurred. Unformed, difficult to categorize and measure, there is a drop in despair, a tolerance of ineptitude and an increased ability to listen without interruption.

Guess the effect would be easier to quantify if I suddenly had this desire to become an ascetic, because the visual is always easier to understand.

The impact within is quite a different equation because it is hidden and comes with confusion and turmoil and endless questions one asks of oneself.

Let me just say that the experience of writing from the outside looking in, is one for which I am truly grateful.

With the agony of self-assessment comes the ecstasy of discovering oneself.

So be it.

Epilogue

It happened. With immense grace and grandeur.

On the day. A dream came true. 14 February 2024 was a millennial moment in every sense. A twenty-seven-year-old prediction by Pramukh Swami was realized. It was his vision projected from a sandy knoll in Sharjah on an evening in 1997.

The submission by his successor Mahant Swami Maharaj that this mandir in Abu Dhabi was God's wish saw grand fruition and made for such a joyous occasion. The aspirations and hopes of thousands of swamis and devotees were realized as the Indian Prime Minister Narendra Modi inaugurated this magnificent house of worship and the promise it offered—of harmony, goodwill and a sense of oneness—to the world.

Truly a message for the next thousand years. So many good thoughts come to mind. In the opening of this house of worship, we celebrate the unity of spirit and the diversity of faiths.

In 2019, at the foundation-laying ceremony, Mahant Swami had said, 'Love, peace and harmony will generate from this mandir and will benefit all of mankind. Harmony is at its best when it is based on the pure intent of wishing good for others.'

'God made this mandir,' said the Swami, 'Harmony can be achieved when we do not expect harmony from others, but instead when we strive for harmony ourselves.'

Wednesday, the fourteenth of February, the truth rammed home. The miracle was unfolding. The mandir was an electrified field, throbbing with palpable excitement. Thousands of devotees from far and near, eager to be integral to this moment, had gathered even before dawn as the consecration ceremony got underway. Later in the day, when India's Prime Minister Narendra Modi would arrive and step out of his car, his first words would penetrate the pages of BAPS history.

'You have brought Pramukh Swami back to life today,' he would say with unbridled emotion as his admiration for what he was seeing in front of him shone in his eyes. At the moment of his arrival, the PM embraced Brahmavihari Swami and said, 'For thousands of years, Bharatvarsh and humanity will be grateful for what you have done. This is an amazing achievement.'

'Humanity is grateful to you, and this moment will remain etched forever, for thousands of years. This mandir truly unites the past and the present and through it, you see the future,' said Mr Modi, encapsulating so succinctly the essence of it all.

Let me just say that everyone of us who will spend time at the temple will be affected in myriad ways—some more forcefully than others—but they will not be the same. Where that impact has its fulcrum lies in the fact that in an Islamic country, there is such a Hindu temple and that two nations, two peoples, two faiths have shown to the world that harmony is not just another word.

It is a mission. And it has been accomplished.

Open to all, a place for learning, a citadel of peace and calm, where humanity is of the essence and spiritual energy abides.

Nothing has changed in the days after the opening. I have watched people transform as they enter the mandir, a self-discipline they impose on themselves because this, this is bigger than they had imagined; this is something else, it requires a different level of assimilation before we can fully comprehend its enormity. They look up at the ceiling and there is a slackening of the jaw, a widening of the pupils, a hush of reverence in the voice . . . surely, God is listening.

He has to be . . . how else could the BAPS organization, its commitment and dedication, have been so richly rewarded? As Swami Brahmviharidas said, 'If there are aliens out there and they are watching us and are trying to judge the earth, may they judge humanity by harmony; our planet by peace, not war. This fourteenth of February 2024 is a defining millennial moment of love, peace and harmony by which posterity shall remember us all.'

Who knows, over the next thousand years another prediction may come true and up there on Jupiter and Mars and certainly the lunar landscape, may flourish oceans of peace and tranquility . . . and another book on another miracle. Till then be with God.